FUNBOARD SAILING

FUNBOARD SAILING

Jeremy Evans

Foreword by Arnaud de Rosnay

Photographs by Cliff Webb

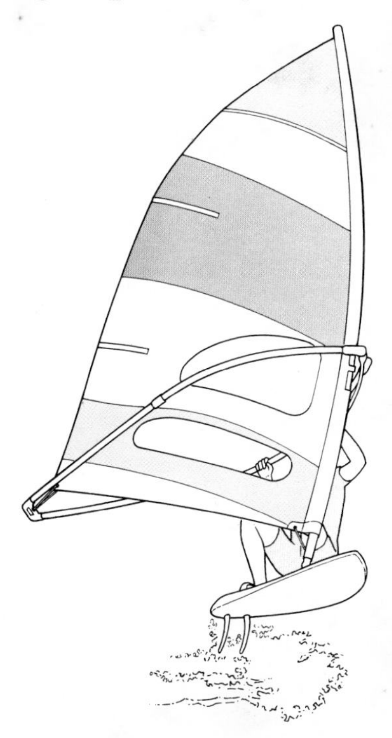

Pelham Books
London

Funboard Sailing was conceived,
edited, designed and produced
by Holland & Clark Limited

Photographer
Cliff Webb

Artist
Nicolas Hall

Designer
Julian Holland

Design Assistant
Martin Smillie

Editor
Philip Clark

Assistant Editor
Christine McMullen

First published in Great Britain by
Pelham Books Limited
44 Bedford Square, London WC1B 3DP

British Library Cataloguing in Publication Data
Evans, Jeremy
Funboard sailing.
1. Windsurfing
I. Title
797.1'24 GV811.63.W56

ISBN 0-7207-1578-4 (paperback)
ISBN 0-7207-1604-7 (hardback)

Phototypeset in Great Britain by
Tradespools Limited, Frome, Somerset

Printed and bound in Hong Kong by
Mandarin Publishers Limited

Contents

Foreword
by Arnaud de Rosnay

In April of 1981 in Maui, Hawaii, I organized the Speed Crossing, a new kind of race which marked a radical departure from the sailboarding events that were the standard at the time. The Speed Crossing was the first professional race in the history of the sport, with cash prizes and trophies. More importantly, it was the first time that a sailboard race had been organized without the rules and restrictions of the IYRU, applied to the sport since its conception (un-fun yachting procedures such as measurement of sails, standardization of equipment, etc). I was trying to lead sailboarding away from the world of conventional sailing and to a freer world of natural, not man-made limits.

In conjunction with the Speed Crossing event, the first 'Expression Session' was held in the waves at Hookipa. With these two events 'Funboarding' was born.

There have been a lot of changes since 1981 and progress can be a mixed blessing. Technically, the evolution of the sailboard has been remarkable. The new sailboard is sleeker and lighter, easier and more fun to use. This evolution has given birth to some organizational problems though, with a return to frustrating regulations and conflicting commercial interests.

But Funboarding will retain its freedom. Although in the past it has been a nice individual ego trip, more and more people are beginning to share their enjoyment by sailing as a couple, using the sailboard to discover our environment from the water. The funboard is like a four-wheel-drive vehicle – it is a performing, adaptable machine. We should encourage a greater understanding of the sea and weather patterns and a respect for the beauty of nature.

Jeremy has witnessed the changes Funboarding has gone through since its conception, and has been instrumental in its continuing development. He's now sharing his insight with everyone interested in knowing more about this remarkable sport.

Introduction

Funboard sailing! You can make it as radical as you like (even as radical as this guy falling off his board) but the ingredients are always the same – good wind and the right conditions, the right equipment and the right techniques.

Finding the place to sail is the first priority. Luckily plenty of nice parts of the world are well-endowed with 15 knot winds. The right equipment is available in limitless quantity and variation. It can range from a 3.6 metre allround-funboard for a sailor with minimum windsurfing experience down to a 2.4 metre sinker for the real expert.

Technique comes last (but not least). The waterstart is not obligatory, but with footsteering, carve gybes and jumps, it opens up the whole spectrum of funboard enjoyment for anyone who takes the time and effort needed to master it. Read on and discover the thrills of sailing a funboard . . . .

HOT

Types of Funboard

'Funboards' cover the widest possible range. At one end of the scale an allround-funboard may measure 3.7 m long with 240 litres of buoyancy and will be suitable for a heavyweight learner. At the other end of the scale a waveriding funboard may measure no more than 2.4 m with around 60 litres buoyancy – definitely a board for really expert sailors who can keep it moving fast in a lot of wind and maybe in big waves as well.

What all these boards should have in common is an affinity for sailing in the stronger winds which produce the most enjoyable windsurfing. This means that they must display a selection of the following qualities.

They should be:

1. *Easy to control in strong winds and/or waves.*

2. *Very fast and needing little effort to control when planing on a beam reach.*

3. *Capable of being foot-steered (that is, steered by banking the board to allow the curved tail to dictate the way it turns).*

4. *Capable of being manoeuvred quickly and sensitively, particularly when sailing on the face of a wave.*

5. *Able to jump clear of the water by using the wave face as a ramp.*

To be worthy of the name, all funboards should possess at least the first three of these qualities. Wavesailing and jumping manoeuvres are more limited to the shorter boards (under three m) – their length is obviously an important factor as is light weight and low volume which makes them so different to sail.

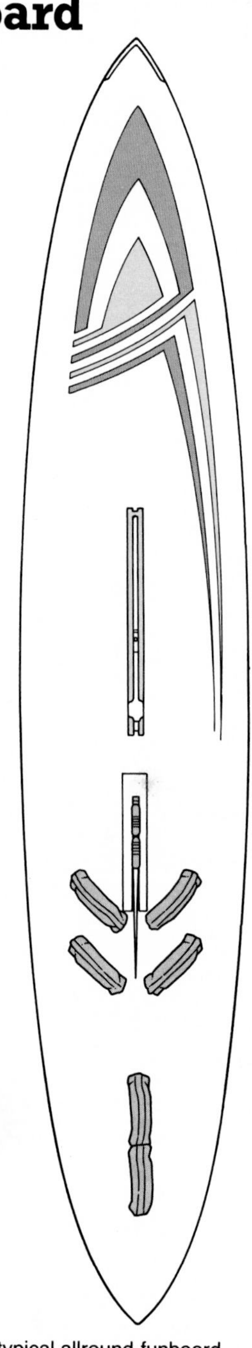

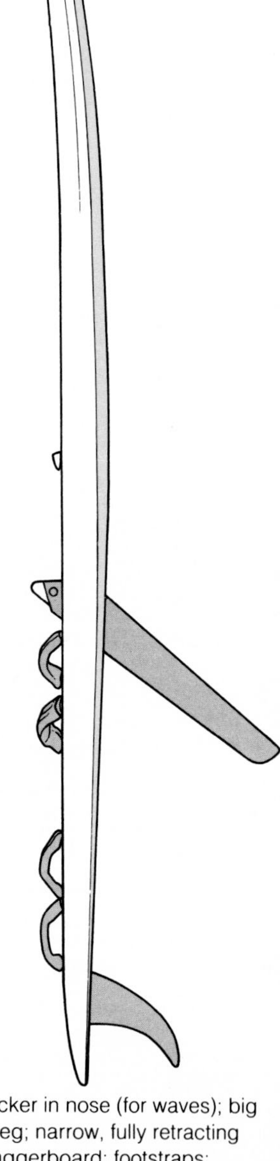

A typical allround-funboard
3.7 m is a popular length; maximum volume about 230 litres; pintail with flattish bottom; rocker in nose (for waves); big skeg; narrow, fully retracting daggerboard; footstraps; adjustable mast track system.

Allround-funboards

An allround-funboard implies a compromise between the qualities of the conventional allrounder and the funboard.

The allrounder may be a fine board to learn on and it's also good for sailing in flat water and light winds of less than Force 4. As the wind becomes stronger the allrounder gets progressively more difficult to control. Gusts make it luff up into the wind and steering becomes unpredictable. Also, without footstraps, the sailor has no firm anchorage.

The allround-funboard preserves the characteristics of the allrounder, primarily the length, breadth and volume which make the board stable.

In addition it will have some or all of the following:

Footstraps so that the feet keep in contact with and can control the board.

Lower overall volume for better control in stronger winds.

A low volume, pintail style tail (it may be rounded pin, diamond tail etc) to allow foot-steering as the board is banked from rail to rail.

A narrow profile daggerboard (controllable on the beats) which is fully retractable for the reaches.

A mast track so that the board can be used full length for displacement sailing, and on half its length (with short board characteristics) while on the plane.

A larger skeg to keep control while planing.

A funboard style rig with relatively short wishbone and a high aspect stable sail for easy handling.

Obviously there are great variations in the design, sizes and shapes of allround-funboards. The biggest may be as long as Division II Open Class boards (3.9 m) with relatively high volume. These are primarily for use on lakes and flat water.

Smaller allround-funboards (around 3.3 m) may have the same fully retracting daggerboard, mast track and tail profile, but are lighter and have less volume. This means they are more responsive and more easily controlled in strong wind conditions.

F2 Lightning 1, a 3.7 m allround-funboard developed from a Pan Am course racing design. In 1984 it was updated to the Lightning 2, taken from the 1983 World Cup design.

High Performance

A specific style of high performance allround-funboard has evolved from the course racing in World Cup funboard regattas (see pages 110–111).

One year's racing prototypes become the next season's production boards. Typical examples include the Mistral Malibu (the design which won the 1983 World Cup), Fanatic Racy Cat, Tiga World Cup, Hi Fly Epoxy Race, and so on.

The design of these boards takes maximum advantage of the three main requirements of a funboard course race, which are:

Beating

The board must go upwind almost as well as a Division II Open Class board. It is sailed on its full waterline length (usually about 3.6 m). The board is banked to leeward so that the thick rail in the middle helps prevent sideslip, along with the daggerboard which may be as much as 70 cm deep.

Reaching

These boards are designed for use with a mast track. With the mastfoot pulled to the back of the track, the board is transformed into a short board and planes on a half, or even just a third, of its waterline length.

It is essential for the designer to know the planing area of the board. The most important considerations are speed and control. Speed is achieved by double and/or single concaves which promote acceleration and keep the board planing. The control is gained by shaping some 'V' into the bottom of the tail, and giving the board low volume hard rails which grip the water in this area.

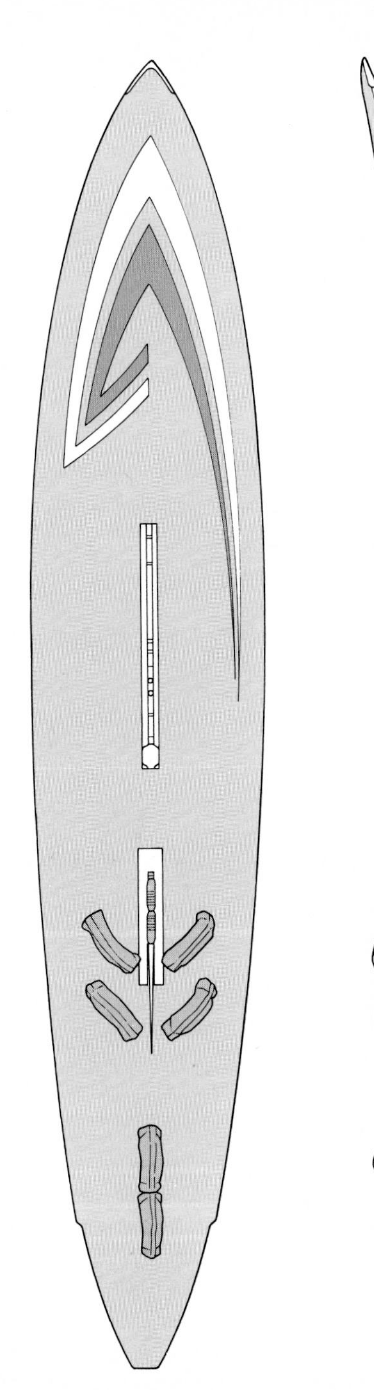

A typical course racing funboard Characteristics: length – 3.55 m is a minimum; volume – may be as low as 200 litres; fairly wide (wingered) tail with double concave bottom to promote lift; lightweight – 16 kg or less depending on construction.

Robby Naish demonstrates beating technique on a Mistral/ Naish World Cup prototype. He allows the board to 'rail', digging in the leeward side to achieve more lateral resistance.

Gybing
Whatever the advertisements may say, gybing a long funboard is not easy. You have to treat it as a short board, standing back on the tail and gybing the board on the area under your feet. The 'V' and low volume, hard-railed tail are important if you are to maintain control.

Construction
In prototype form these boards are invariably custom made from a foam blank laminated with glassfibre.

In production form the manufacturers have a problem maintaining the same weight/ stiffness ratio and the better boards tend to be expensive.

Rigs
In funboard course racing the minimum wind speed is usually 12 knots and sometimes 15 knots. To perform well in these marginal conditions the long funboards need big, powerful rigs which may be difficult to handle upwind but which give the necessary speed on the reaching legs of the course.

Many of the European-made boards are equipped with 6.5 sq m or occasionally seven sq m sails as standard. Whilst this size of sail is suitable for lake sailing in 12 knot winds, alternative smaller sails should be considered for recreational use and easy handling on the open sea.

Short Boards
Short boards are the essence of funboard sailing, and can be recognised by the following characteristics:

Short Length
The longest short boards are around 3.2 m – the shortest may only be 2.2 m. A rule of thumb is that the shorter the board, the more wind it will need and the more skill required to sail it, though obviously volume and shape need to be taken into consideration.

Light Weight
Short boards are extremely light indeed, usually weighing less than 11 kg. A custom built board may be as little as 5 kg.

Volume
Many manufacturers stretch the truth about the volume of their boards. The maximum short board volume is likely to be around 160 litres, while a really short board may be only 60 litres. Generally speaking, less volume means better control in strong winds but the board will require really expert handling. A higher volume short board can be sailed in light winds, but will start getting out of control (bouncing out of turns, spinning out and simply getting blown around) as the wind increases.

No Daggerboard
These boards are designed for reaching, so a daggerboard is an unnecessary weight and encumbrance. To get back upwind you have to close reach with the board banked to windward, relying on speed to get you home. The upwind performance of these boards is at best mediocre.

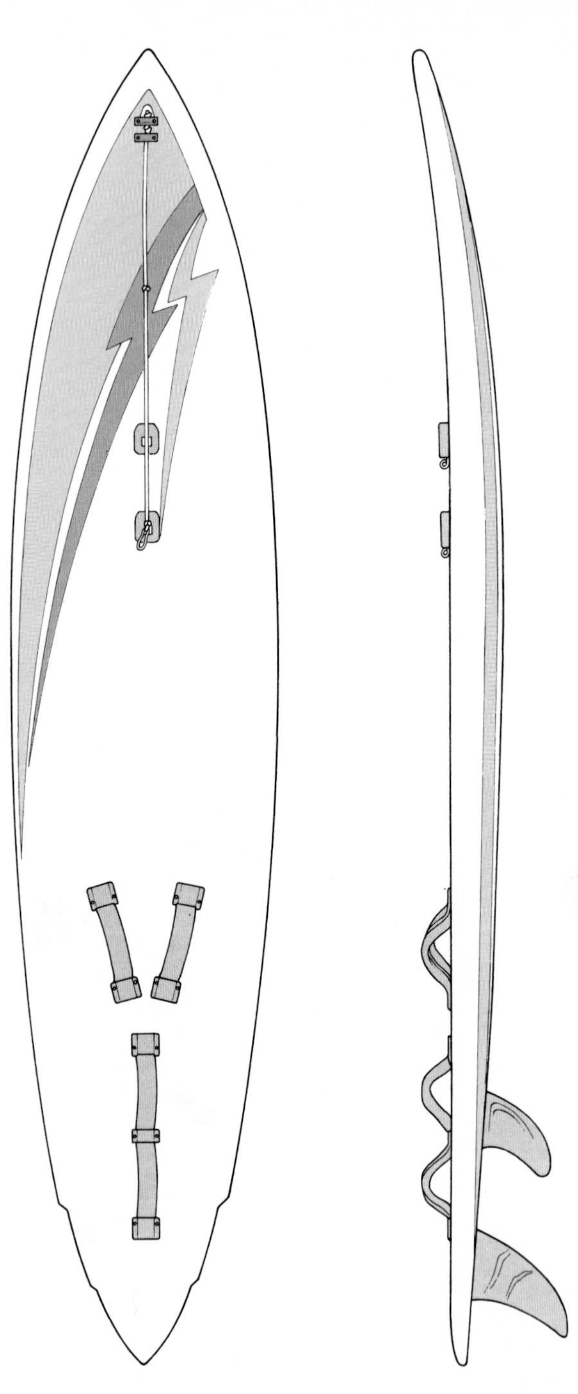

Typical short funboard features found on a marginal: length – around 2.95 m; volume – about 120 litres; outline shape – basically a pintail (but may have wingers, swallowtail etc); no daggerboard; skegs – single or tri-fin.

Types

Short boards can be divided into several categories:

The floater actually floats! It has enough buoyancy to support the rider and can usually be uphauled. Minimum length is likely to be around 3.1 m – any shorter and it will become very unstable, however high the volume.

The marginal has enough volume to be uphauled and sail back home if the wind drops. But usually it should be waterstarted. Length is around 2.9m and it can be considered a transitional board between floater and sinker.

A sinker doesn't have enough buoyancy to support the rider's weight properly unless it is planing. It must be waterstarted, and if the volume is very low a fairly advanced technique is required to get it going.

In European conditions the sinker is always identified with strong winds (20 knots plus).

Hawaiian Sinkers

In the big wave conditions found in Hawaii, it is quite usual for expert sailors to be able to use sinkers in light winds, relying on speed on the wave face to keep the board on the plane.

A gun may be a floater, marginal or sinker. It is based on a surfboard design which has the wide point of the board well forward to create a long, drawn out pintail. The advantage of this is that the long, thin shape with plenty of 'V' stays in control at high speeds since very little of the bottom is in contact with the water. Also the long pintail keeps control in wide arc, high speed turns.

The asymmetric, like the gun, can also be a floater, marginal or sinker.

Construction

Although the major manufacturers produce short boards in polyethylene and ABS, the favourite material is glassfibre (the cheapest to manufacture), with epoxy or polyester resins. A significant number of these boards are custom made.

Short boards offer jumping, manoeuvrability and speed. Once you can handle the waterstart (really vital to the enjoyment of funboard sailing) and the carve gybe, the short board is normally much better mannered and easier to control than the allround-funboard.

Funboard Design

How are funboards designed? In some cases the designer may sit down at a drawing board to draft the plans for the outline and the templates for each section. But it's much more likely that he'll start by working with a block of foam, shaping it with a variety of tools (see pages 120–121) until he is satisfied with the design.

Shaping

In this respect funboard design is part art, part imprecise science. It certainly owes a great deal to two decades of surfing and surfboard shaping.

There are many factors which govern the design of a funboard. They must all be considered and blended together so that the resulting board looks good, matches the needs of the rider it's designed for, and will perform well in the prevailing conditions.

Outline

The factors which influence outline (plan view) are the tail shape and position of the wide point in the board.

If the wide point is fairly far back, it will create a wide tail shape with accentuated curves that will encourage the board to plane in marginal conditions, and gybe or turn in a tight, slow arc.

If the wide point is well forward, the tail shape becomes a drawn-out pin with very little curve, which will encourage the board to turn a wide, fast arc.

The wider the board, the greater its planing surface, and in marginal conditions wide boards offer good performance. In higher winds their extra surface area will drag, and the tendency to bounce and skip will be much greater than on a narrow board. Responsiveness and turning ability are also less in a wide board.

Narrow Tails

Narrow tails are slow to plane, but with adequate wind the length of the planing area is extended. This immerses more rail, increases lateral resistance and reduces the load on the fins so that only a single fin is required.

A multi-channel design helps planing, but makes a lot of work for the shaper.

Tail Shape

The tail of a funboard should be very thin with hard rails that sink and grip when the rider turns the board. There are many different kinds of funboard tail shape.

Squashtail

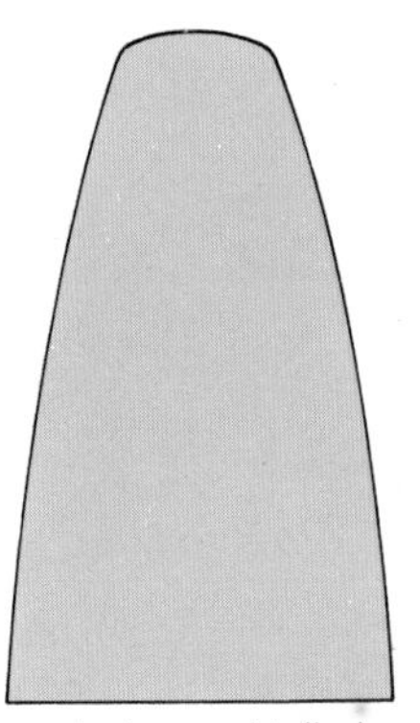

The rounded squashtail gives more volume and tail area than the pintail. It's normally found on slalom and World Cup race boards which need instant acceleration and lift at the cost of easy gybes.

Pintail winger

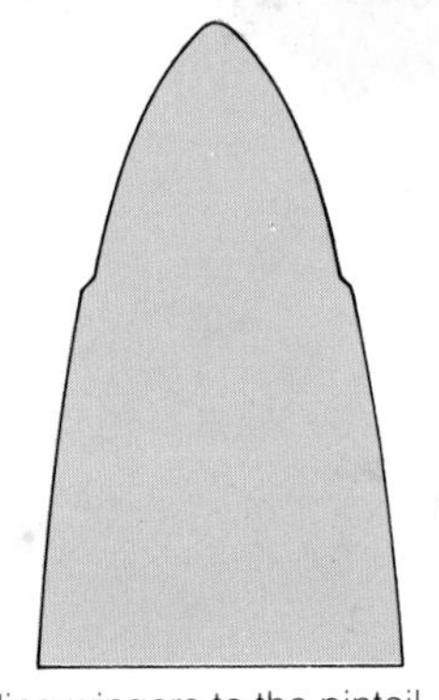

Adding wingers to the pintail gives a wider tail area which promotes earlier planing. The wingers are shaped to grip the water during turns and are aligned with thruster fins. Some boards have two sets of wingers, but it's all more work for the shaper.

Pintail

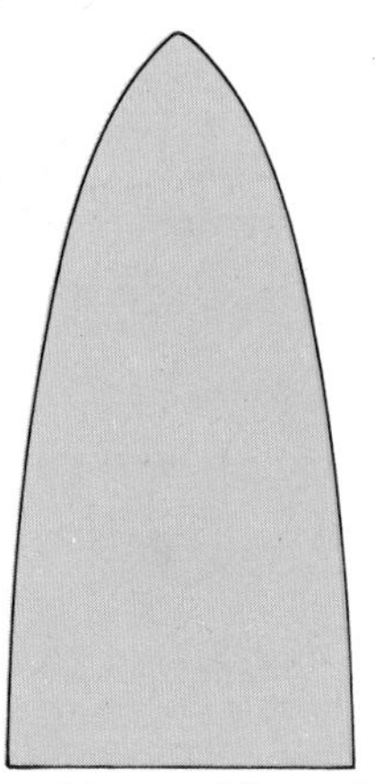

The pintail is one of the easiest tails to shape and has a profile that encourages wide arc, high speed gybes.

It is found mainly on guns and slalom boards which are designed for maximum speed. A major disadvantage is its low volume and narrow width which makes marginal wind planing very slow.

Squashtail winger

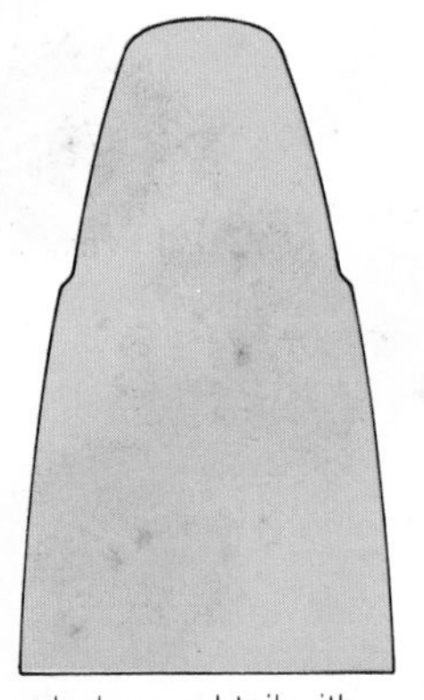

A rounded squashtail with wingers helps to cut the area and improves gybing.

Swallowtail winger

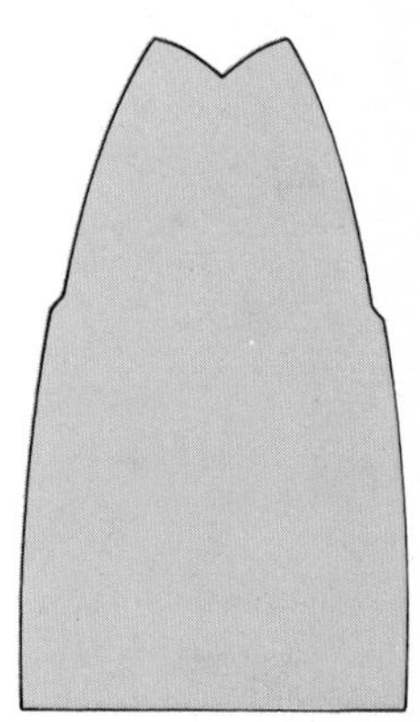

The swallowtail winger turns the pintail into two small pintails with extra tail area and volume for quick planing – allied to the stable handling characteristics of the single pintail. The addition of wingers is optional and will depend on the whims of the designer.

Diamond tail

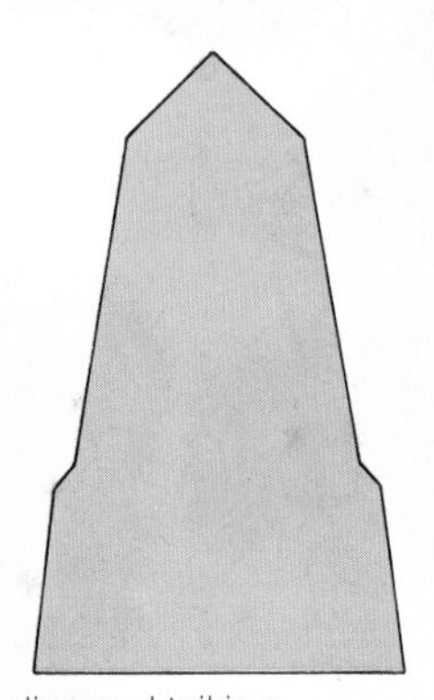

The diamond tail is a compromise between the squashtail and pintail, usually found on slightly longer allround-funboards but losing popularity in recent years. Once again the addition of wingers is optional and may or may not help the design.

Nose Rocker

The amount of scoop or rocker needed at the nose depends on the type of sailing required. For instance, a speed board for flat water requires very little nose rocker, although a certain amount is necessary to prevent nose diving in waves.

Tail Rocker

Tail rocker is a crucial factor in funboard design as it has a major influence on manoeuvrability. Too much (ie a banana-shaped design) and the board will be very slow. Having no tail rocker at all, however, would be equally unsatisfactory. Although the board would plane earlier in moderate conditions, in strong winds the large planing surface would offer too much water resistance and the board could not go any faster.

Slight tail rocker, which cuts the wetted surface and aids manoeuvrability, is what's needed.

Rail Design

Rail design incorporates subtle variations in shape throughout the length of the board to achieve the best performance. It is, however, usually a compromise. For example, a hard rail may trip the board, and cause the tail to bounce and skip when the clean water release fails to press the board to the water.

A full soft rail fails to promote water release which presses the board to the water. But fullness would make acceleration sluggish if used for the whole length of the rails.

A rail with maximum fullness at $\frac{3}{4}$ depth (achieved by the tuck) lets the water flow up to that full point before it releases. Therefore it gives traction without sluggishness and the rider gains speed through water release at $\frac{1}{4}$ height, while the fullness of the rail helps prevent skipping when on the turn.

Rails

The rails are the edges of the board. They flow all the way from the nose to the tail. The rail shape alters considerably from one end of the board to the other.

At the tail, the rails are shaped thin (low volume) and hard, so that they can sink and grip the water in turns.

Moving forward, the rails become fuller, rounder and softer in the middle section of the board, aiding flotation and stability, and giving the board lateral resistance.

In the front part of the board the bottom edge of the rail is frequently cut away to give a tucked-under edge which separates and releases the water cleanly.

Rail profiles showing water release

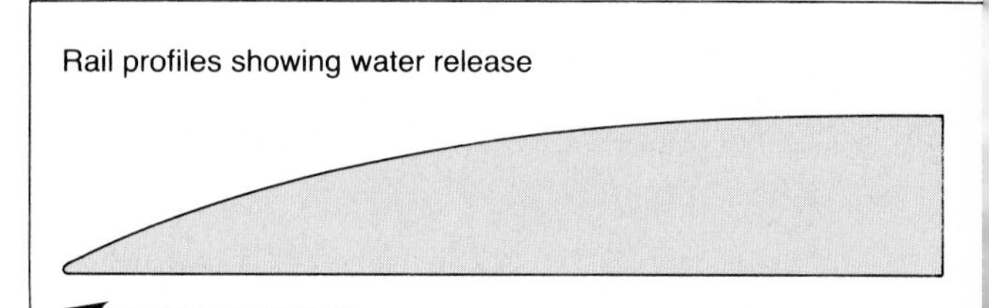

Low, hard rails release water cleanly, but the board may trip on its nose as the rail digs into the water, while the tail may bounce and skip without any grip.

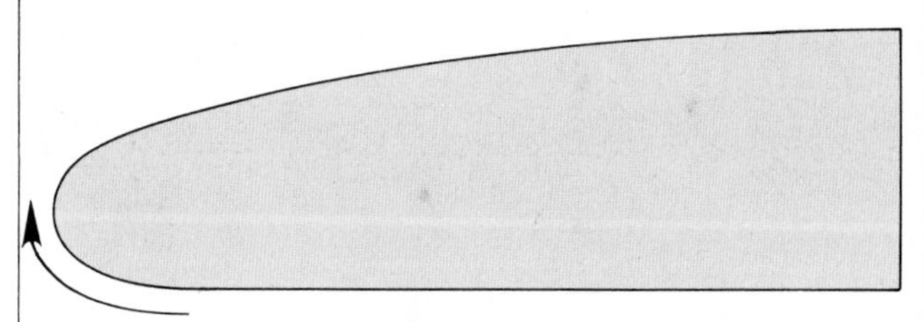

A full, soft rail encourages water to flow up round the rail and hugs the board to the water, encouraging stability but making the board sluggish and unwilling to jump.

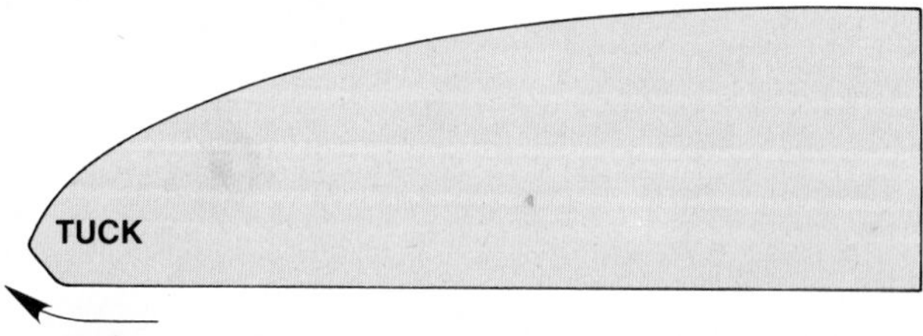

The compromise shape has a 'tuck' which allows the water to flow up around the first quarter to the fullest point. This gives traction without sluggishness (the combination of the soft and hard rails) for maximum speed in a straight line and control in the turns.

A modern wave board shaped and made by the famous partnership of Harold Iggy and Rick Naish. You can see quite clearly how the position of the wide point influences the profile and tail shape.

Bottom Shapes

With adequate wind a flat bottom board is fast, but it will give a hard ride, rattling along like a tea tray, and with nothing to grip the water.

For these reasons it is usual to have some 'V' at the tail. This cushions the ride and gives some grip on the water. Having 'V' further forward tends to make the board bounce from chine to chine. It is more usual to have a slight roll in the bottom, a triplane (a flat bottom which is slightly angled at either side for displacement sailing), or more recently a double concave.

The double concave channels air under the board to promote lift. It usually features a 'V' in the middle which makes the board directionally stable. In some cases the boards may have multi-concaves (or channels) which are designed to have the same effect. These, however, present problems to the builder.

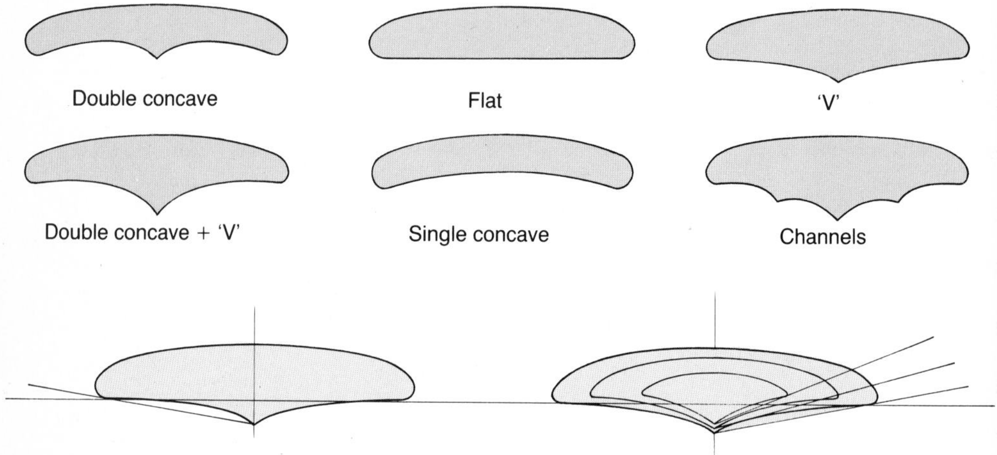

The double concave was around for many years in the surfing world before it broke through into windsurfing with Hansi Fichtner's World Cup designs of 1983. From that point the concept has been developed in a variety of ways with different designers looking for the best compromise solutions, with the tuck playing an important role in water release at the rail.

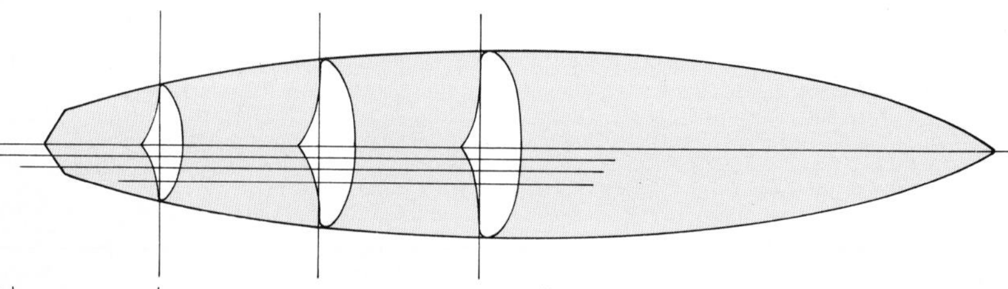

The double concave gives dynamic lift for early planing, while the 'V' helps stability and manoeuvrability. However the shape must vary throughout the length of the board. The 'V' and concaves are usually most pronounced in the middle sections. At the nose they may be incorporated into a single concave which will give extra lift to prevent the nose sinking when it overtakes a wave.
At the tail the double concave usually tapers to a flat 'V' for manoeuvrability and stability. Tail shape also helps determine planing characteristics.

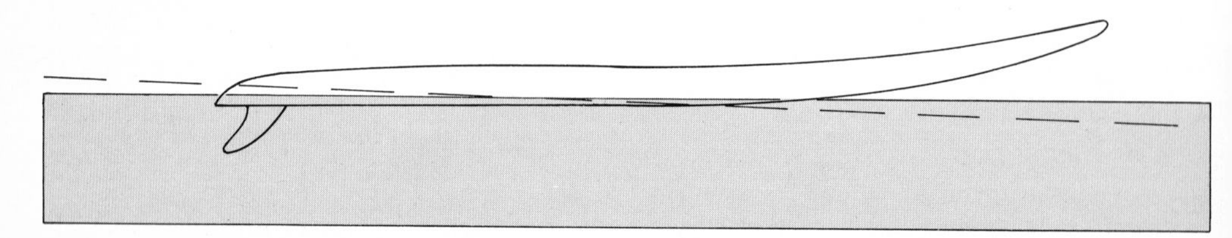

Volume

The amount of foam in a board dictates its buoyancy, while the foam flow (where the foam is positioned in the board) dictates the situation of the buoyancy.

Volume is an important consideration for the designer since it influences how easily the board will plane (hence the exceptionally high volume of Division II boards). It also affects how the board will behave in certain difficult conditions and dictates whether the board will be a floater, marginal or sinker.

Apart from its outline shape, the latter consideration is also influenced by the weight of the sailor. A board may be a floater for a sailor of 70 kg but for a heavyweight rider of 100 kg it's certainly a sinker! This is an important feature to bear in mind.

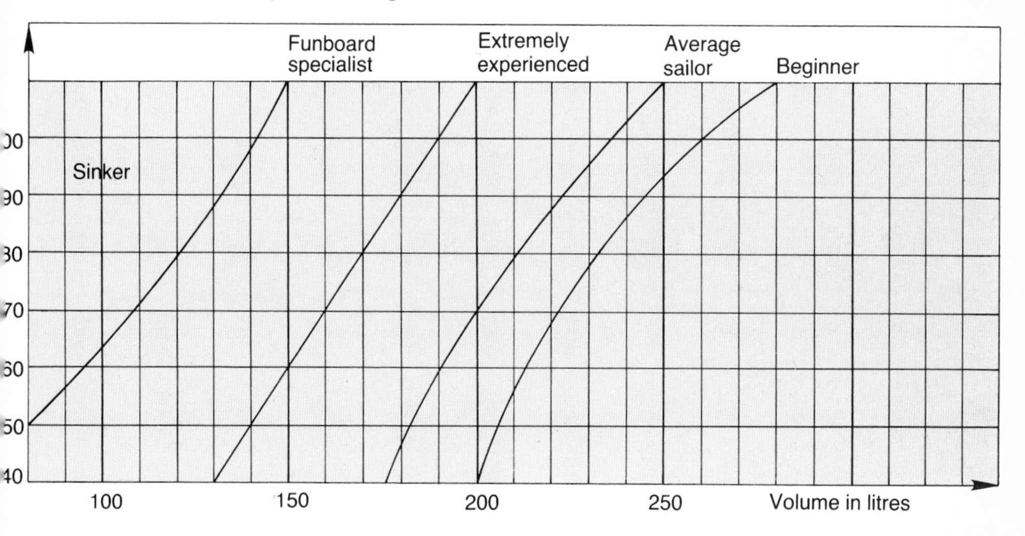

What volume for your weight? Look for you own weight on the left side of the graph and draw a horizontal line until you reach the shaded area which most clearly matches your own requirements. Then look on the bottom line for the minimum volume. Obviously there are many other considerations.

Below: Despite their similar volumes, these three boards will all have very different sailing characteristics suitable for varying weights and skills.

Asymmetrics

The asymmetric is designed purely and solely for wave-riding and the theory behind its shape is relatively simple.

Bottom Turn

As you come down the far side of a wave, you need to make a bottom turn. This is a turn away from the wind, often involving a gybe on to the other tack, to enable you to head back up the face of the wave.

Since you are coming down the wave, the bottom turn will be made at very high speed, and you need maximum control from the board. The best tail shape for this situation is a narrow drawn-out pintail with a thin rail for slicing into the water and holding the board in the turn.

Cutbacks

Having made the bottom turn, you sail back up towards the crest (or lip) of a wave. Here you will need to do a top turn (or cutback) turning the board away from the lip to descend again on the fast part of the wave.

This is a tight turn (sometimes a gybe), made when the board is decelerating, so there is a risk of the tail sinking. This will stall the board with potentially disastrous results. To prevent this happening the tail needs to be wider and shorter which will maintain low speed planing throughout the turn.

A wave ride continues with a repeated sequence of bottom turns and cutbacks along the face of the wave. The tail shape requirements for the two turns are entirely contradictory, and a conventional symmetrical shape board is a compromise between them.

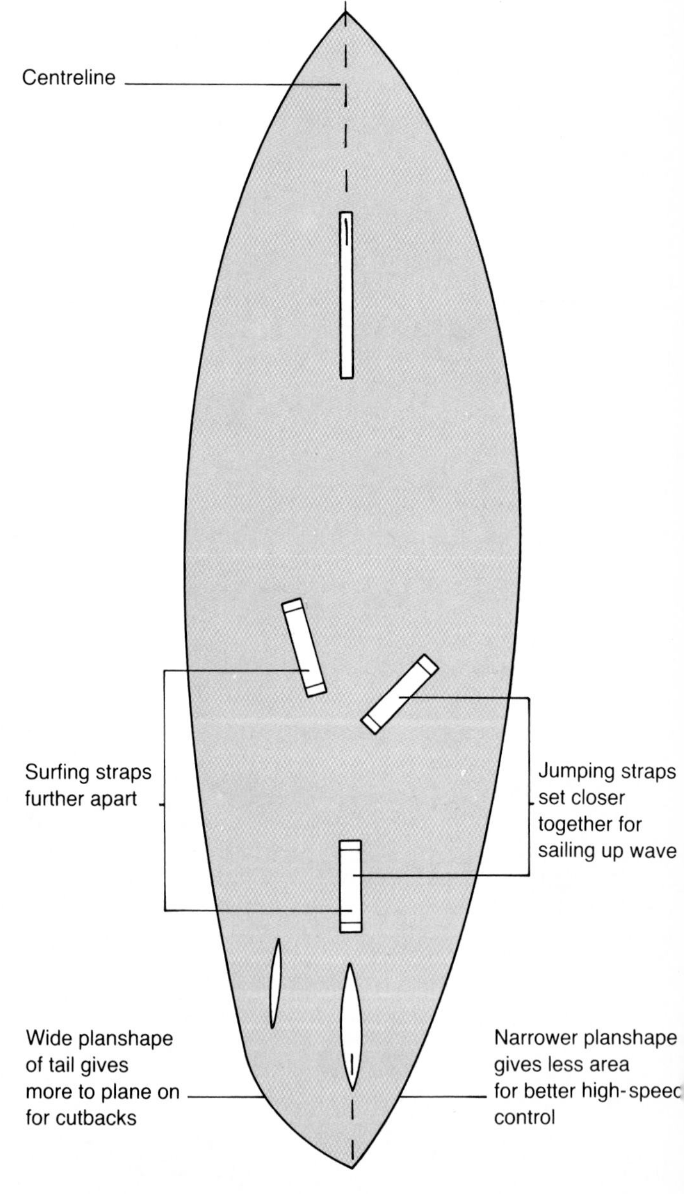

Above: The cutback profile is on the left-hand side of the board with small thruster fins. The bottom turn profile is on the right side with the large main fin. The obvious disadvantage of the asymmetric is that it is only of use in consistent conditions which are found in a few places like Hawaii.

Below: Deck view of another board designed for the same consistent wind and wave conditions. The surfing straps are set well apart for descending the wave on the port tack, before making a bottom turn and heading up the wave on starboard tack ready for a cutback.

Construction and Materials

The fundamental problem with funboard construction is to find the right mixture of volume, weight and stiffness – all at a price the market can bear. Achieving the correct mix is problematic for the manufacturer and, as a result, several slightly different methods of construction have developed as makers have sought to find the solution.

There are in fact five main methods of construction:

Polythene Rotomoulding

This is the original manufacturing method used by windsurfer makers. The polyethylene skin is hard-wearing but the board is relatively heavy and this makes it a less suitable material for funboard construction.

Manufacture commences with a bag of polyethylene granules being poured into a steel mould. The mould is then heated in the rotomoulding machine, which rocks and rolls it until the melted polyethylene coats the inside surface of the mould.

Once the mould has cooled, the polyethylene skin, looking like a limp white sausage, is removed. It is placed in a 'foaming jig' (another mould which is the exact shape of the board) and polyurethane foam is injected in two-part liquid form. This expands and solidifies to form the solid core of the board.

The board is then removed for the fixing of the various fittings and decals before dispatch.

Polyethylene Blow Moulding

Blow moulding is a newer, more sophisticated method of manufacture for polyethylene boards. A blow moulding machine is considerably more expensive than one for rotomoulding. So, in order to satisfy economies of scale, the process is only used by major manufacturers who can sell large numbers of boards.

The polyethylene granules are dropped into a hopper and heated. When the plastic is sufficiently liquid, it is extruded as a long tube (rather like a drainpipe) which is lowered into a vertical mould. The mould is clamped shut, and compressed air is blown in. This inflates the plastic tube until it takes the shape of the inside of the mould.

The polyethylene skin can then be removed and the manufacturing process continues along similar lines to rotomoulding.

Vacuum Forming

Vacuum forming uses plastic of the ABS family. There are two main manufacturing processes in current use:

1. Single sheet

Each sheet of ABS plastic is fed into a machine. It is heated and then sucked down on to a mould (the vacuum). One sheet is sucked down to make the bottom of the board and the other sheet is sucked on to the mould which makes the top of the board.

Excess plastic on each skin is removed. Then any necessary inserts (daggerboard case and footstrap reinforcements etc) are bonded to the insides before the skins are placed in a foam jig to be filled up with polyurethane foam.

Most boards made by the single sheet method have the top skin overlapping the bottom, rather like a biscuit tin lid. The seam is 'caulked' with a flexible sealing compound. Less sophisticated boards use a plastic H-strip to hold the two halves together but this may not stand up sufficiently to the rigours of funboard use.

2. Twin sheet

The twin sheet method of vacuum forming is appreciably different in that it commences with the manufacture of the core.

Most manufacturers using the twin sheet method opt for foam cores of polystyrene. These are considerably lighter than polyurethane but they cannot be injected in liquid form.

The polystyrene core is made in a mould which heats and crushes polystyrene granules (rather like tiny ping-pong balls) until they amalgamate and are formed into the correct shape. This is then ready to be coated with the ABS plastic.

The core is placed in a machine with a sheet of ABS plastic above and below it. The plastic is heated until it is soft. At this stage a mould clamps down from both top and bottom, cutting off the surplus plastic and sealing the ABS skin round the core.

The great advantage of this system is that there is no seam between the top and bottom half of the board.

Which ABS?

Understanding different manufacturing techniques is complicated by the many fancy trade names which are in use. This is particularly true of ABS and you will encounter some of these names being used by

major manufacturers:
ASA is the material being used primarily by Sailboard and F2.
Polycoren is used by Mistral.
Copex is used by Fanatic. Copex '84 is mixed with polycarbonate to stop the yellowing which is caused by exposure to sunlight.
Lexan polycarbonate ABS is employed by Klepper who use the single sheet method. Each sheet is prelaminated with one layer of ABS and one of polycarbonate.
LCS is used by Mistral. The skin material is a mixture of ABS and polycarbonate. But the manufacturing method is somewhat different as the polystyrene core is covered in epoxy glassfibre and the LCS forms the outside skin.

Dangers

ABS has an unfortunate characteristic in that it is sensitive to changes in temperature. In particular it becomes brittle and susceptible to breakage if subjected to extreme cold. This could be a problem if a low volume funboard was being used in big wave conditions. Mistral went so far as to point out the dangers of breakage on their Tarifa board in temperatures of below 50°F.

Care should be taken when exposing any board to extreme temperatures. In particular, hot sun may lead to discolouration and even delamination of the skin.

Pop-Outs

The system of glassfibre 'pop-out' manufacture (a term which sounds derogatory but isn't) is used by most of the British funboard manufacturers, who are based mainly in Devon and Cornwall. Chapter, New Waves, Limited Edition, Vitamin Sea, Circle One, etc, have been able to build on their surfboard experience to produce low price boards which are both up to the minute and reasonably light and strong. They all also produce custom boards, some of which are the prototypes and plugs (to make the moulds) for the boards they put into production.

Pop-out manufacture starts with glassfibre cloth being laid in the top and bottom moulds. Varied thicknesses are used to suit the structural requirements of the board. The glassfibre is then laminated with a liquid polyester resin catalyst. This transforms the cloth into the glassfibre skin.

The top and bottom skins are bonded together (usually by the biscuit tin method), placed in a foaming jig and filled with polyurethane foam.

The board is then taken out and sprayed with a custom airbrush finish using cellulose car paint. Alternatively, the board may have a straightforward single colour gel coat which is sprayed into the mould before the glassfibre cloth is laid in position.

Exotics

Glassfibre is the most usual skin material, but a builder may opt for a more 'exotic' material with a better strength to weight ratio. Two well-known materials are carbon fibre and Kevlar, but in practice these tend only to add to the price of a short board without necessarily improving its structural qualities.

Another possibility is to use a 'sandwich' skin. Two layers of glassfibre cloth sandwich either a thicker layer of very dense, hard foam or a cloth which has properties to help spread the resin (such as Firet). The sandwich is invariably stronger than straightforward layers of glassfibre.

Compression Formed Boards

The weight of any board is divided between the core and the skin. A polystyrene core will always be lighter than one of polyurethane and similarly an epoxy resin makes a stronger skin laminate than polyester. However, there are problems in working with epoxy and polystyrene:

1. Epoxy is a difficult and dangerous material to work with.
2. Moulding polystyrene cores is capital intensive (too much so for the small manufacturers) and polystyrene is much weaker than polyurethane.

The major manufacturers evolved 'compression forming' as the best way to produce epoxy boards that are light and strong but, unfortunately, they are rather expensive. Mistral, F2, Alpha, Hi Fly, etc all use variations of this technique.

They start by moulding the core from the polystyrene granules. (In the case of Alpha the core is composed of an outer polystyrene case filled with polyurethane).

The top and bottom moulds for the board are sprayed with a hard outer gel coat (usually white) before the core is covered in the glass cloth. It is quickly wetted with epoxy resin and placed in the bottom mould. Then the top mould is clamped down and it is 'baked' in an oven to give a super hard, perfect cosmetic finish.

Epoxy Repair

With skill and experience it is possible to repair virtually any damage to the skin or core material of a board. Minor impact damage is relatively easy to put right but tread carefully if you are considering tackling anything bigger.

There are three types of board repair: minor skin damage; major skin damage which may require replacing foam; and major damage to both skin and foam. All of these can be dealt with by non-experts as long as the right materials are obtainable.

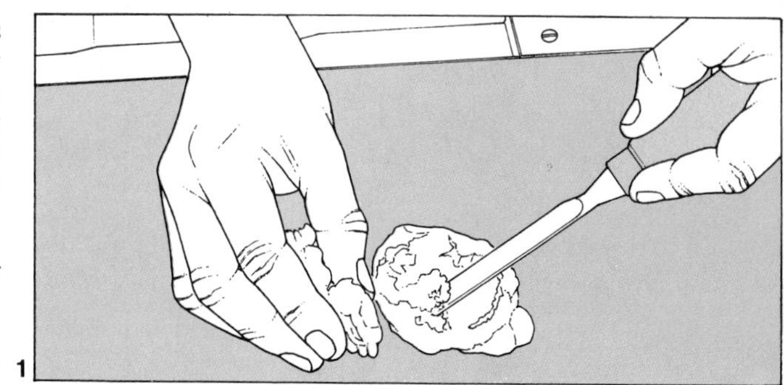
1

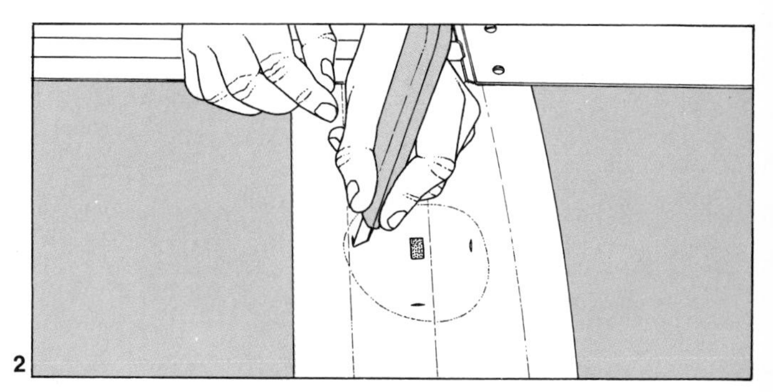
2

Golden Rules

Funboard damage is invariably most easily repaired with epoxy. Before starting work, remember the golden rules:

1. The repair area must be clean, degreased and 100% dry.

2. Instructions and mixing ratios must be followed exactly.

3. Some materials are toxic or unpleasant. Allow for ventilation and beware of fire.

4. Ambient working temperature must be at least 20°C.

5. Don't fill large holes with resin. The heat build-up will cause an even bigger hole in the foam – use PU foam.

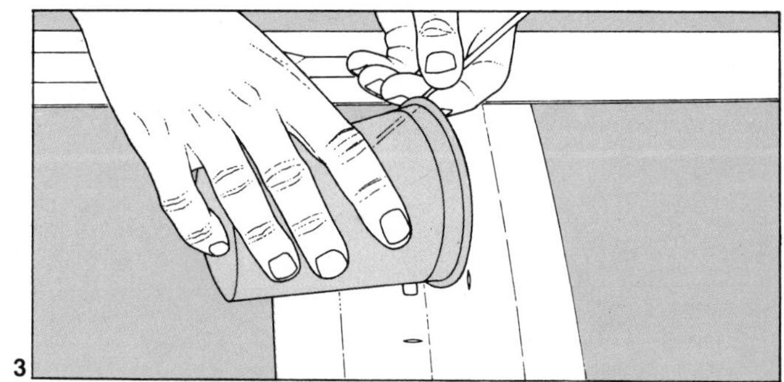
3

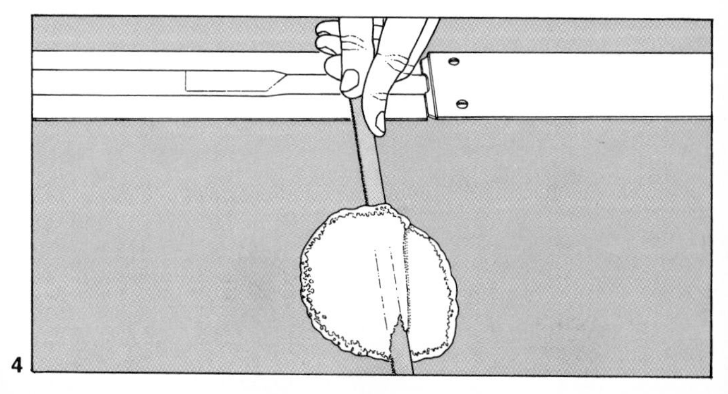
4

1. Remove the damaged skin, and then dig out the wet or damaged foam using a knife. Make the hole perfect so that there are no sharp edges, and then roughen the surrounding skin using a file or sandpaper.

2. Cover the repair area with layers of adhesive tape. Cut a central hole and smaller air holes.

3. Prepare two-part PU foam, and pour it through the hole. Cover the centre hole with tape and allow excess foam to escape through the smaller holes.

4. After the specified hardening time, remove the tape and cut the top surface off the foam with a hacksaw.

5. Sandpaper the foam until it's level with the underside of the skin, and then use a hacksaw blade to make a 5 mm horizontal slit all round beneath the skin.

6. Mask round the repair area, and stipple epoxy resin on to the foam up to the edges. Drop on CSM, keeping it wet with resin, and build up the depth until you can tuck the CSM into the 5 mm slit with the hacksaw blade. Continue building up the depth until it's level with the outer skin.

7. When it's very dry, sandpaper to 1 mm below the outer skin. Then apply a polyester filler. Leave it to harden. Then file down the top surface, taking care not to damage the surrounding skin. You can then wet-and-dry it with medium grade paper until the filler is smooth and flush with the surface. For the best possible finish apply another coat of cellulose car body putty, and rub down with fine grade wet-and-dry.

8. You can then paint the area with matching colour using a brush. Alternatively, a spray gun gives a much better finish for paint on a non-slip surface.

Main materials required are epoxy resin, CSM glassfibre, PU 2-part foam, polyester filler, cellulose putty and acrylic paint.

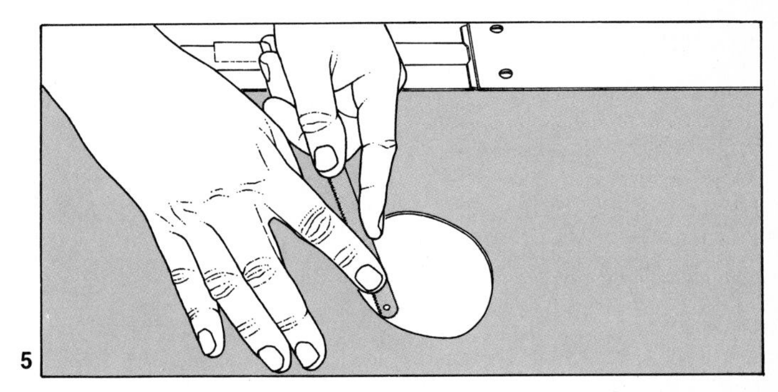
5

6

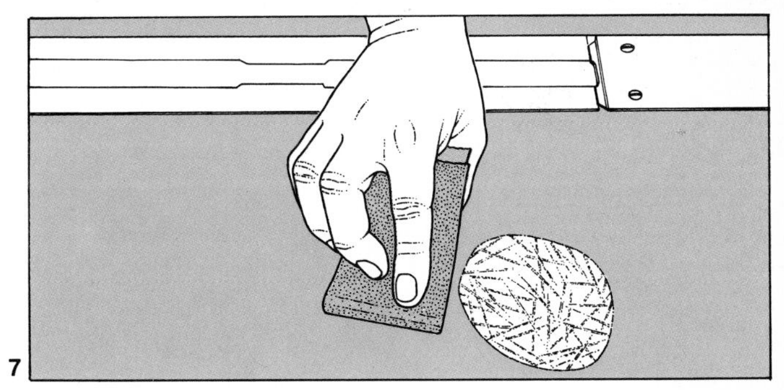
7

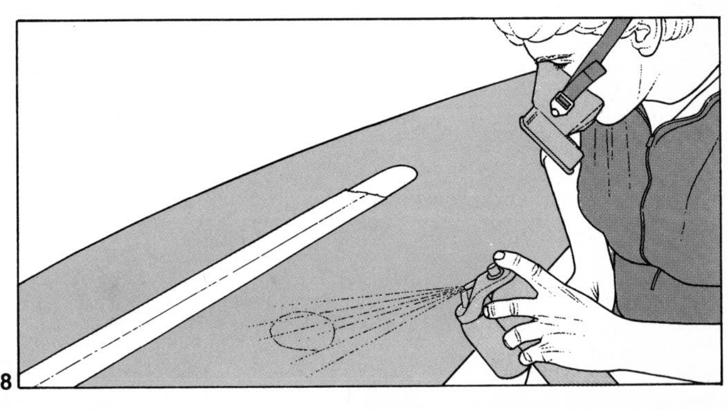
8

Accessories and Fittings

Harness Technique

The invention of the harness liberated windsurfing from being a sport where you hung on to the boom with gritted teeth until your arms gave out and forced you to fall off. However, the harness must be used with caution. Before relying on it a sailor should be capable of handling the board in Force 4 winds. In the wildest kinds of wave riding and jumping conditions it can be dangerous to hook on with a harness.

Harnesses are expensive and so it's important to choose the type you need. If you want to learn to waterstart you

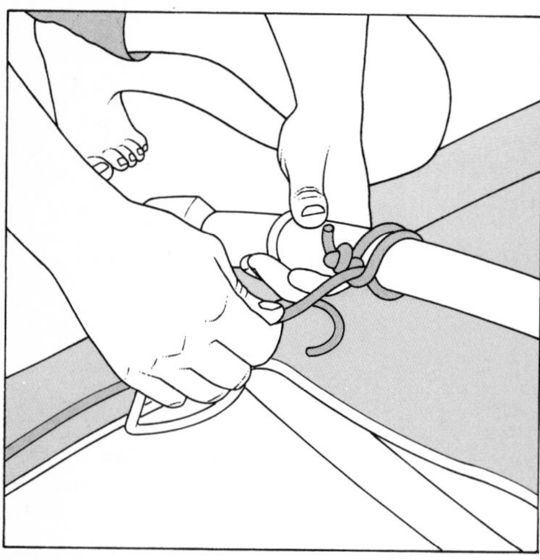

Harness lines should be pre-stretched Terylene, usually 5 mm or thicker. Buy enough for several lines and carry the rest as spares in case a line breaks while you're sailing.

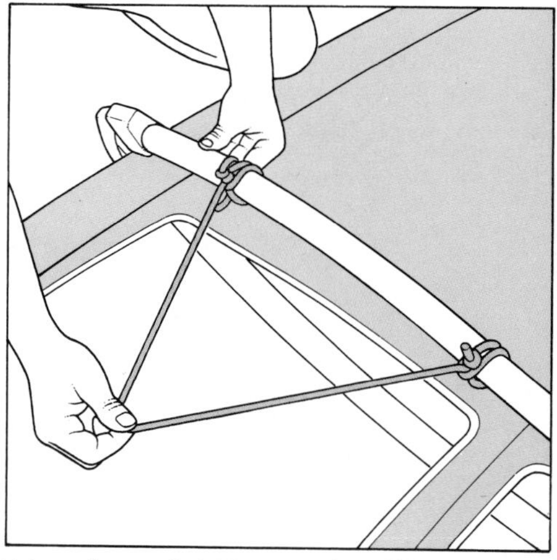

Using a figure-of-eight stopper knot. This is an easy way to attach harness lines to the booms. Either end can be loosened and adjusted for the optimum position.

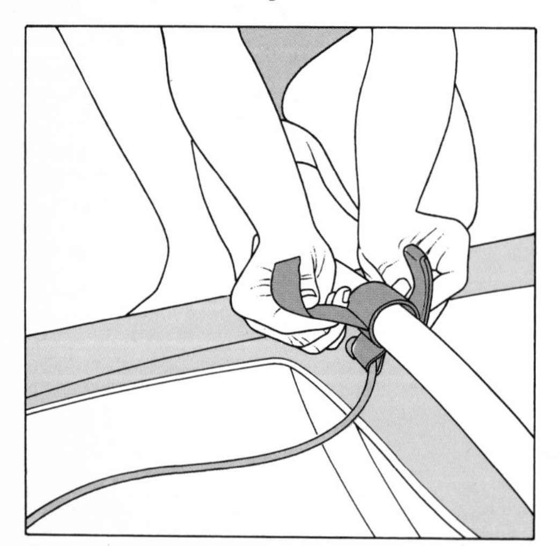

Many harness lines are sold in made-up packs with Velcro tabs to attach them to the booms. It's a quick and easy method, but rather more expensive than buying a length of line.

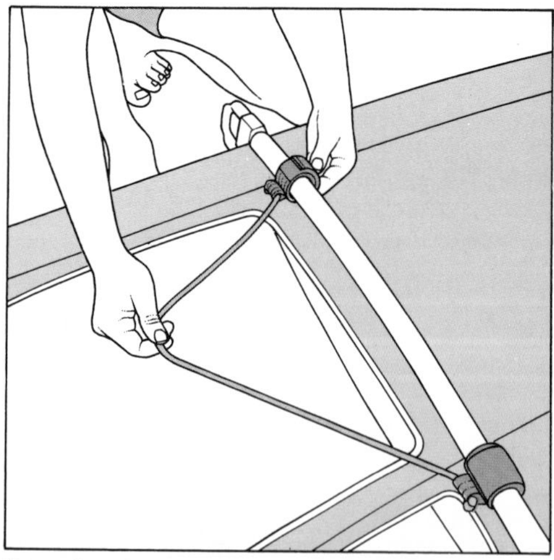

The point where you hook in should be directly between the attachment points, with the pull on your harness corresponding to the Centre of Effort in the sail.

Your hands should fall naturally close to each end of the line. The boom height should be set so that you're in an easy, straight-backed stance.

should go for a high buoyancy type that keeps you floating around in the water. Make sure it's a tight fit which doesn't ride up over your body when you are submerged. Generally, the harness with four straps beneath your ribs attached to the hook or spreader is best at preventing riding up.

Minimum buoyancy

Once you master the water-start, a harness with minimum buoyancy and bulk is better for sailing in waves, and the only kind that will permit effective swimming.

Most contemporary harnesses are fitted with spreader bars that are designed to spread the load across your chest with most of the pull taken by your back.

Spreader Position

It is a common mistake to set the spreader too high. It should be placed low down, closer to the waistline than the chest, in a position where it is comfortable and won't budge.

Harness Lines

On the old style of allround board it was necessary to have harness lines about one metre long because of the length of the boom. On a modern funboard the boom is so much shorter (under two metres for preference) and the sail much more stable with a controlled Centre of Effort. A 55 cm harness line should be quite ample.

Plastic Tubing

Short lines have the advantage that they are less likely to flip over on to the wrong side of the boom. However, if this is a problem, cover them with narrow plastic tubing.

Clothing

Neoprene Drysuits

Over the past few years, the quality of all windsurfing equipment has improved dramatically.

In clothing the major advance has been the new smoothskin neoprene drysuit (right) which originated in the UK in 1982.

With neck, wrist and ankle seals (or integral socks) this type of suit should be completely waterproof. The single-lined neoprene (generally 5 mm thick) is very warm. Although it is tight it is very stretchy, which makes it ideal for funboard sailing and use in the waves.

Some manufacturers bond a loose Goretex neoprene top on to a neoprene long john (near right) for greater freedom of movement and 'breathability'. Others use all neoprene for maximum warmth (far right). Both types are excellent for cold water use though correct fit is vital.

Below: If it's not too cold it's best to sail with bare feet. You get better 'feel' and if the deck is slippery you can try wax.

Some sailors advocate the Okewind style of shoe (left) for use with neoprene socks on a drysuit. The problem is that their bulk makes it hard to trim the board or use footstraps.

If you have to wear boots they should be based on neoprene for warmth but should be light and supple for easy movement.

Below: If the vulcanized covering on a wishbone hurts your hands, try canoeists' light nylon and leather gloves. Few gloves help in cold weather but the Spartan style dry glove or a neoprene mitten are the best options.

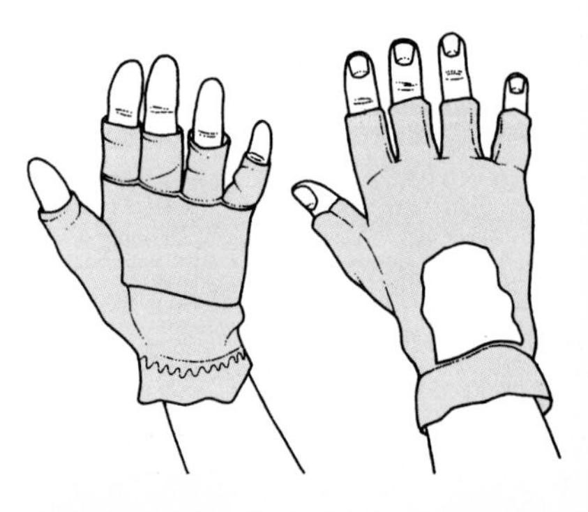

Like the smoothskin drysuit, the 'steamer' style of wetsuit (right) is a revolutionary improvement in windsurfing clothing.

All the seams are glued and then blind-stitched – it's a stitch which only goes halfway into the neoprene and therefore no water can penetrate. With a tight fit at neck, wrists and ankles (use ankle straps), the result is a suit which lets in very little water, and the little that does get in stays there, heating up around the wearer's body.

The steamer is a one-piece blind-stitched suit. The same stitching can be used on the same style of suit with short arms or short legs for warmer weather.

Different thicknesses of neoprene are available for winter (6 mm) and summer (3 mm) use. The thickness necessary will depend on the temperature of the water where you sail.

Two features to look out for in a steamer are stretchy smoothskin arms (so your arms won't get cramped) and a pair of neoprene flaps over the zip to form a seal and prevent water running in and out.

Footstraps

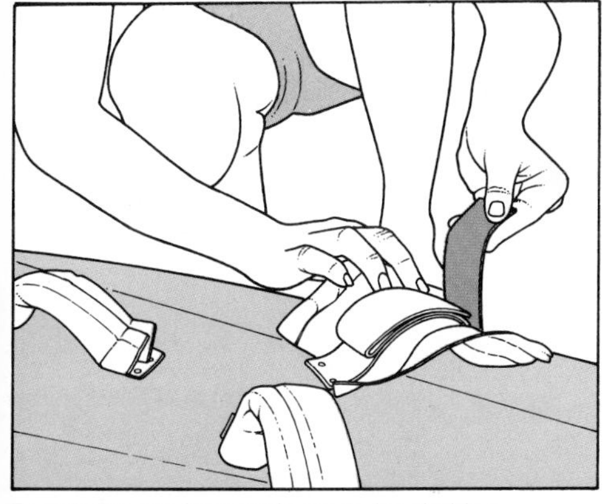

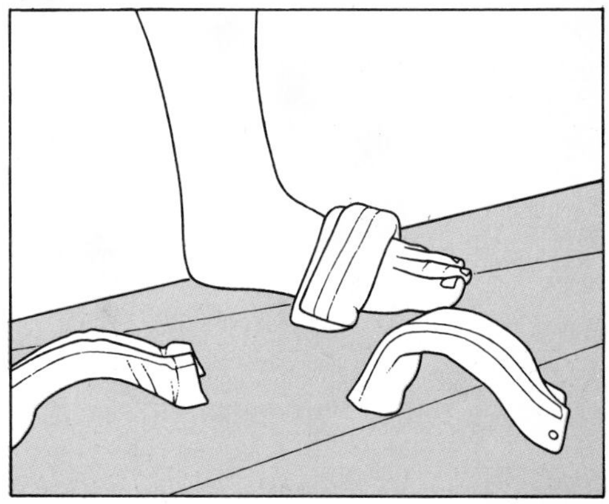

Footstraps are frequently made by clothing manufacturers. The best are soft and well padded but rigid enough to stay up when wet. They should be fully adjustable and only your toes should poke through. If the strap is too big you risk serious ankle injuries if your foot slides through.

Mastfoot

All the bits and pieces that add up to a mastfoot assembly (illustrated right) make it an amazingly complex piece of gear. It is also prone to coming undone and breaking, so it pays to check it all regularly and keep it in good working order.

Always keep the assembly well lubricated. If you fail to do so, the nuts which hold the components together will rapidly become corroded and difficult to move. This can make it impossible to remove the bottom fitting, which often has to be changed when you want to swap to a different board.

In the middle of the assembly is the rubber powerjoint. This can be a vulnerable and high-risk part of the mastfoot. Rubber powerjoints first appeared in the late 1970's and breakages were common, with either the bottom or top shearing off and leaving the rider with an unattached rig.

However, design has since improved and more recent examples have an integral steel cable which runs through the powerjoint from bolt to bolt. This makes a total breakage unlikely but it is still advisable to leash the mastfoot to the nose of the board.

The greatest variation in mastfoot assemblies comes in the bottom fitting. Most manufacturers use different track or plug systems. Very few of these are compatible when boards are changed.

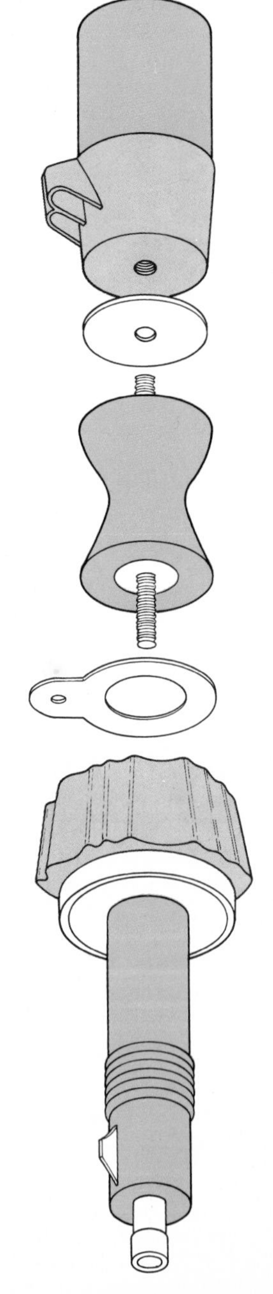

Below: Many shorter funboards use a simple polycarbonate fin box as the mast track. There are a variety of bottom fittings designed to screw into the fin box nut (the one shown is made by the Dutch manufacturer Canton), and unlike fancier mast track systems they are generally compatible. The only disadvantage is that the foot is fixed when sailing.

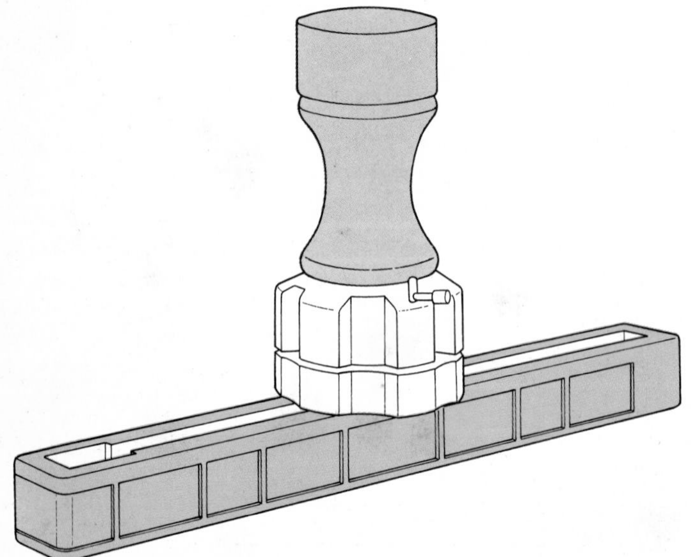

Daggerboards

Most funboards of over 3.2 m in length have a fully retracting daggerboard system. Shorter boards don't have room and would become unbalanced with a dagger. They rely on stronger winds, speed, and the lateral resistance of the fins and windward rail to get them upwind.

All funboard daggerboard systems are similar to the design pioneered by Allgaier in West Germany. The high aspect plastic daggerboard retracts into a cassette which fixes through the top and bottom of the board. There is a gasket to prevent water surging up through the case.

Unless you are racing, the funboard dagger should be either fully up or fully retracted. It should be right down when you are beating upwind and retracted on every other point of sailing. Even if only the tip protrudes, it will send the board into a wobble when it is on a reach.

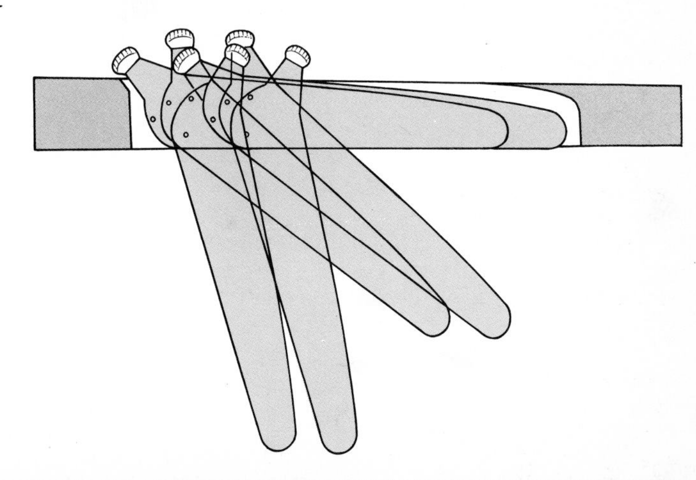

Right: Some daggerboard systems have two positions in the case for different length daggerboards. You use the shorter daggerboard when there are stronger winds.

Below: The daggerboard must be easy to retract or push down with a swift movement of your foot. At the same time it must be quite rigid in its case and stay down when put in the down position. Many cases allow for adjustment. A stiff blade performs best but is not often found on production boards.

Fins

How Many Fins?

Wide tails have a greater planing area than narrow tails, and therefore require a greater fin area to aid lateral resistance. As a rough guide, a tail that is less than 27 cm wide (measured 30 cm from the stern) will only require a single fin, while anything wider will need three.

However, you can't have a simple rule of thumb on the number of fins, and the volume and profile of the board has to be considered, as well as its use. For small waves or chop three fins are most suitable; for wide arc high speed turns single fins are the norm; while speed, slalom or race boards almost always use a single fin – they are not designed to carve tight turns and the single fin gives much less drag.

In some cases boards are being fitted with four or more fins following surfboard trends. However, their usefulness is as yet unproven and they are a minority fashion.

Thrusters

'Thruster' fins are the little ones on either side of the main fin. They are usually foiled on the outside and flat on the inside, with the fin boxes angled inwards so that straight lines drawn from each one would meet at the nose of the board.

Length

For single fin boards in big waves a fin depth of 22–25 cm is normal. On three-fin boards the thrusters should be one-third to one-half of the depth of the main fin – if it is any more the outer fin will tend to hydroplane during carved turns and make handling difficult.

Fin Positions

Moving fins forward in the boxes 'loosens' the board so that it becomes more manoeuvrable and less directionally stable. Moving them back has the opposite effect.

Only experience will tell the optimum fin position so you should experiment. *It is normal to move three fins as a set.*

Ventilation

A fin produces side forces by means of decreased pressure on one side. If this process causes air to be sucked down the fin from the surface of the water, the fin ceases to work efficiently. This is 'ventilation' (spin-out) which usually occurs at speeds approaching 20 knots.

It is normal (though incorrect) to use excessive area to combat the spin-outs that result from ventilation. In fact, spin-out is more likely caused by the following: a poor rig with the CE too far back; the mastfoot too far back which decreases the board's wetted length; the footstraps too far

The theory is that ventilation starts at the fin base, so the Foot fin has a large tip and narrow base area. In practice it works extremely well in preventing ventilation.

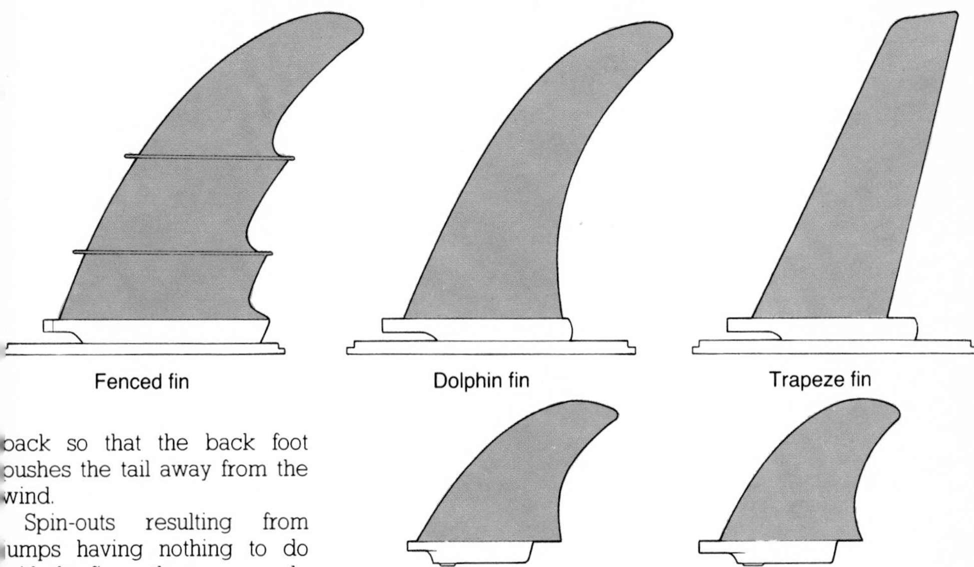
Fenced fin
Dolphin fin
Trapeze fin
Thruster side fins

back so that the back foot pushes the tail away from the wind.

Spin-outs resulting from jumps having nothing to do with the fins – they are purely due to landing with the tail downwind of the nose.

Safety

The trailing edge of a moulded fin emerges razor sharp from its mould. A blunt tip and trailing edge don't detract from a fin's performance – always sand off all the sharp edges.

Very little is known about the ideal fin. Many are designed because they look nice, but a lot soon get discarded.

The basic requirement is that the foil should be a constant curve from leading to trailing edge with maximum thickness one-third of the way back. Any flat area will promote turbulence.

The conventional dolphin shape fin evolved from surfing and is free from trimmings and gimmicks. The curved leading and trailing edges are responsible for hydrodynamic efficiency, and foiling is the most important factor. The straight-edged version – the trapeze fin – enjoyed a period of popularity: it was considered to be better upwind, but otherwise inferior.

Fenced fins (top left) adapt the dolphin shape with horizontal fences and a modified trailing edge. The fences are there to prevent ventilation, and in practice they are slower to ventilate, and much easier for the less experienced sailor to correct spin-out without the great loss of speed which occurs with the conventional dolphin.

The strongest moulded fins are made of Lexan polycarbonate – a translucent coloured plastic. However better fins are made by hand in glassfibre.

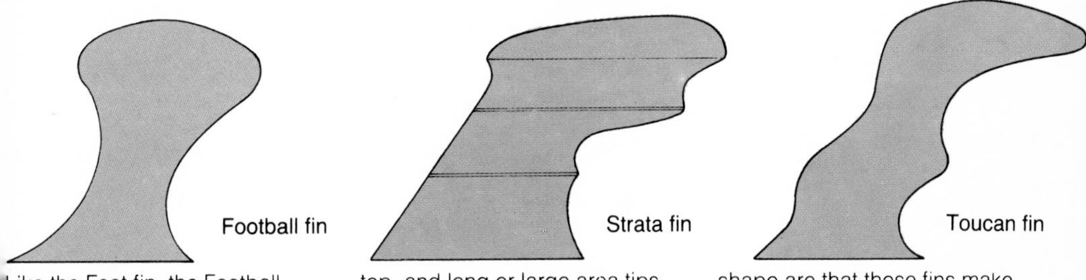
Football fin
Strata fin
Toucan fin

Like the Foot fin, the Football, Strata fin and Toucan have all been developed to combat spin-out, with a narrow profile at the top, and long or large area tips with deep penetration. The disadvantages in comparison with the conventional dolphin shape are that these fins make the board stiffer and less easy to turn, and are also prone to picking up weed.

Installing Fins

Most boards have the universal style of fin box which will accept a wide range of fins from a variety of manufacturers – the top brands such as Multifin (Australia), Fins Unlimited (USA), Chapter (UK), etc are generally compatible.

The square nut is slipped into the fin box **(1)** which can be a fiddly job – use the blade of a screwdriver to get it on to the grooves. Slide the back end of the fin through the notch into the box **(2)** and position the front end so that the bolt locates directly over the nut. You can then screw it down **(3)**, but before it's tight slide it to where you want it in the box.

Generally, if it's near the tail, the board will travel straighter (it's 'stiffer'), and if it's at the front the board is more manoeuvrable ('looser').

If the fin is a loose fit it will vibrate and have an adverse effect on the board's performance. In most cases you can assume that the manufacturer has made a poor job of Installing the box. It is always wise to check on this before buying a board. If you have a loose fin, try wrapping tape round it to obtain a tighter fit.

1

2

3

Custom Fins

Most fins are moulded from a translucent, coloured plastic called Lexan polycarbonate. The plastic granules are poured into a heated hopper and melted; the liquid is injected into a steel moulding tool, and not long afterwards (40 seconds for a small thruster) out pops a fin.

Custom fins are very exclusive and notably different. Apart from being much stiffer than Lexan, they have a weight penalty and you can expect to pay at least twice the average price.

Custom fin manufacture is skilful, time-consuming and labour-intensive. A panel is laminated with 29 or more layers of variously coloured glassfibre cloth. Once the panel has cured, the fin shapes can be cut out **(1)** with an electric saw. Each fin is then foiled **(2)** with a power grinder until it's the right shape – measured by the expert 'eye' of the craftsman.

The fins are then completed with gloss spray, fine sanding and polishing, before the fin goes in for testing in the fin box **(3)**. It can take up to ten days to produce a batch from a panel and this accounts for the high prices – but look at the beautiful colours!

1

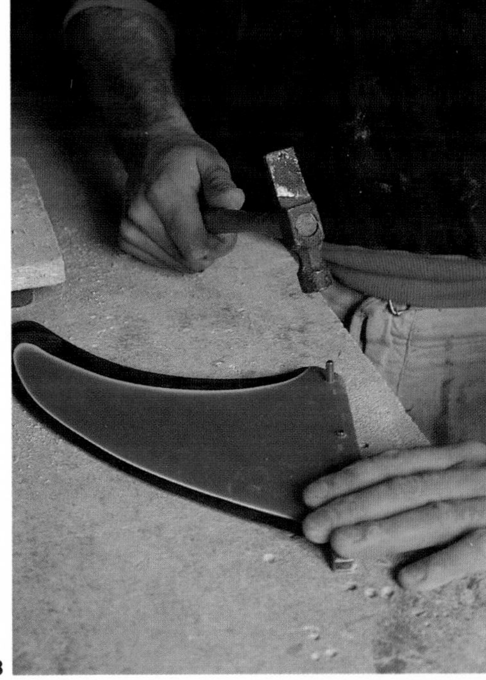

3

Rig and Sails

Masts and Booms

The most popular mast material is glassfibre, though for high-performance sailing stiffer materials, such as aluminium or carbon fibre, are often preferred.

The stiffness of the mast must be suitable for the sail you are using – if you're not sure, ask the sailmaker. It must also be the right length (about 15 cm longer than the mast tube) and with the new generation of high aspect sails, that frequently means masts of five metres and more.

If your mast is too short you can increase the length with an extension. But you must remember that this may distort the bend characteristics of the mast and interfere with the set of the foot of the sail. To avoid this, the extension should fit flush into the base of the mast.

Booms also need to be stiff so that they keep the sail in a consistent shape whenever a gust hits.

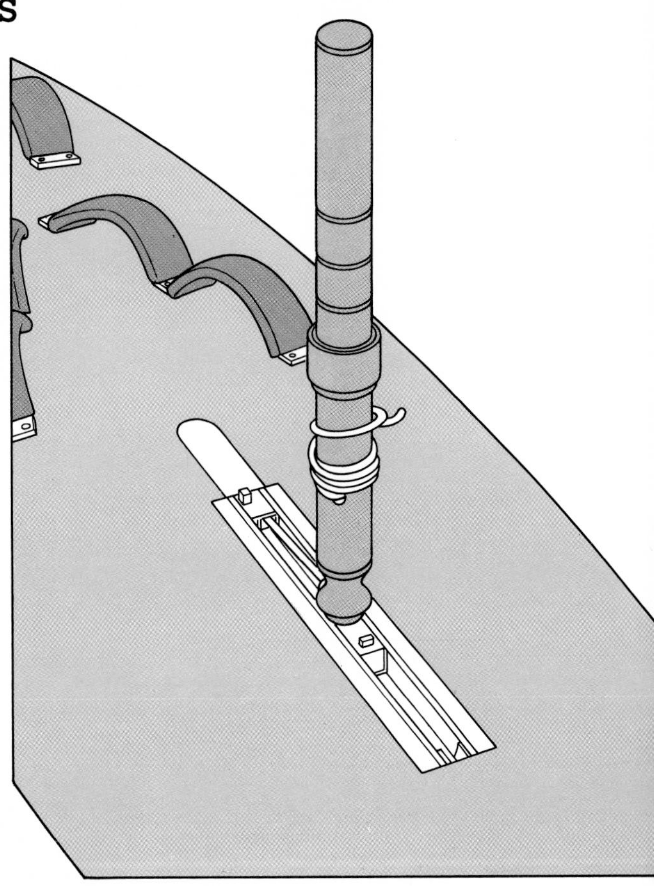

Above: An adjustable mast extension can add up to 30 cm mast length. Many of these extensions are very susceptible to salt and corrosion and clogging or jamming with sand. They need careful cleaning and maintenance and should be removed from the mast after use.

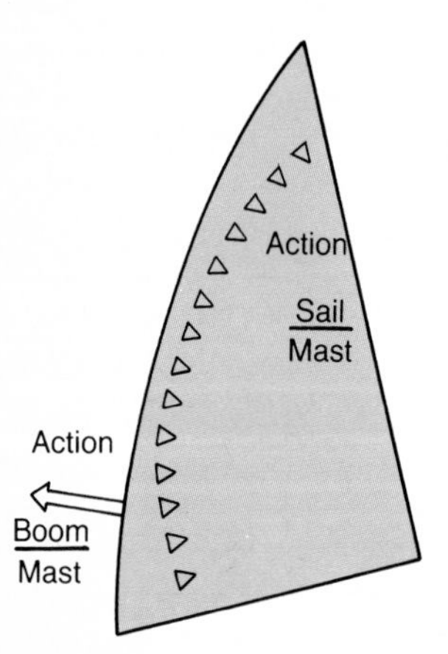

Above: All masts bend, and this diagram shows the forces induced in the sail. The luff must be cut in a curve to suit the bend of the mast.

There are a variety of types of adjustable boom. Some telescope (watch out for corrosion) while others (below) have removable sections to change the length. The best tend to be the most expensive and include North, Windsurfing Hawaii, MK, Mistral and Fanatic.

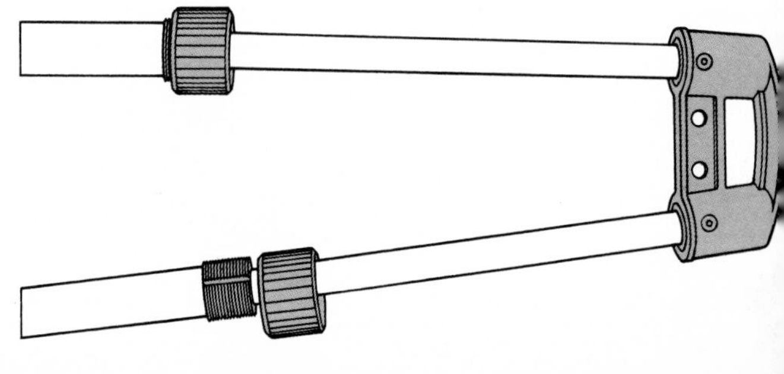

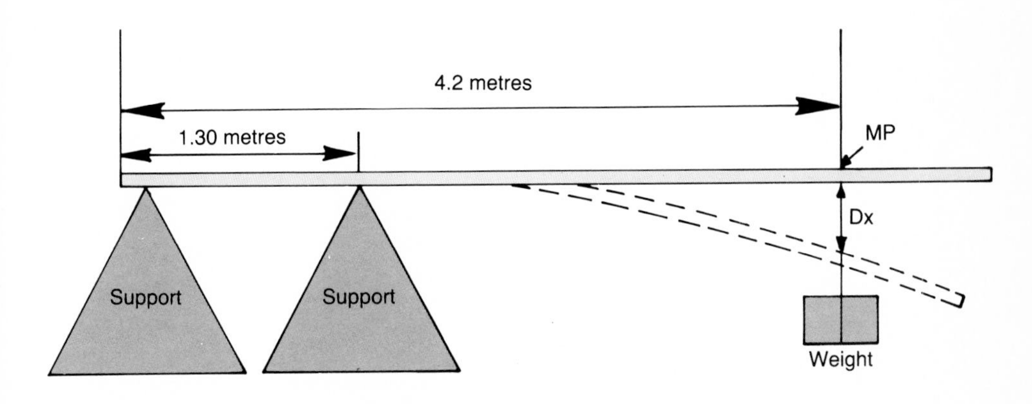

MP = measurement point Dx = deflection under load

Above: The stiffness of a mast can be measured. To do this, you support the mast across two trestles, one at its base and the other 1.30 m along its length. At a distance of 4.20 m measure the height of the mast from the ground. Then suspend a weight from this point and re-measure the mast's height above ground.

You can then work out a 'stiffness value':

Stiffness =

$$10 - \frac{\text{Deflection (cms)}}{\text{Weight (kg)}}$$

This method gives a surprisingly accurate indication of stiffness.

Speed Sail

When there's not enough wind to go on the water, you can have a lot of fun on a speed sail – so long as you have a suitable beach.

The speed sail is essentially an enlarged skateboard with damped 'trucks' steering the front and back wheels. You bank it into turns, changing tacks with the conventional carve gybe or fancier duck gybe. The trucks can be adjusted to suit your technique and the conditions – loosen them for slalom manoeuvrability and tighten them for straight line control at maximum speed.

The speed sail is used with a conventional rig, though the biggest sails used are about 4.2 sq m with 1.6 m booms. This is quite enough for plenty of speed in Force 2. Beyond that the governing factor on speed is your own nerve!

Mast Track

The adjustable mast track first appeared on boards at the 1982 Pan Am Cup in Hawaii. Since that time self-respecting performance orientated all-round-funboards have switched to having a track that can be adjusted while you're sailing along out on the water.

The track makes a board into two boards. In its forward position it is designed to be used with the daggerboard fully down while the sailor uses the whole length of the board to displacement sail upwind.

The Centre of Effort is well forward which will counteract any luffing effect without having to rake the rig right forward, making for a well-balanced and easily handled board.

As soon as an allround-funboard bears away on to a reach, the daggerboard must be fully retracted if the board is going to stay under control.

The effect will be to move the Centre of Lateral Resistance back towards the tail of the board, and to keep in trim the mastfoot must be moved to the back of the track.

This change has several beneficial effects. The board will begin to plane on its back half, giving it the effective length of a short funboard; the rig can be held more upright, giving more power from the sail and, with the CE moved back towards the tail, the board will become much more manoeuvrable and easier to gybe.

Obviously there are variable factors which will affect the way in which you use the mast track. The size and shape of the sail, the wind and sea conditions and your own sailing style will all influence the correct position for the mastfoot.

The only answer is to experiment until you feel that board, rig and your sailing style are working in harmony and then just lie back in the harness.

Types of Track

There are many different types of track supplied with boards and they all have their good and bad points. Some are easier to use with bare feet than boots and vice versa (it depends on the size of the foot pedal). Some are prone to clog with sand, corrode in salt water or warp in the sun, whilst the design of others is so poor

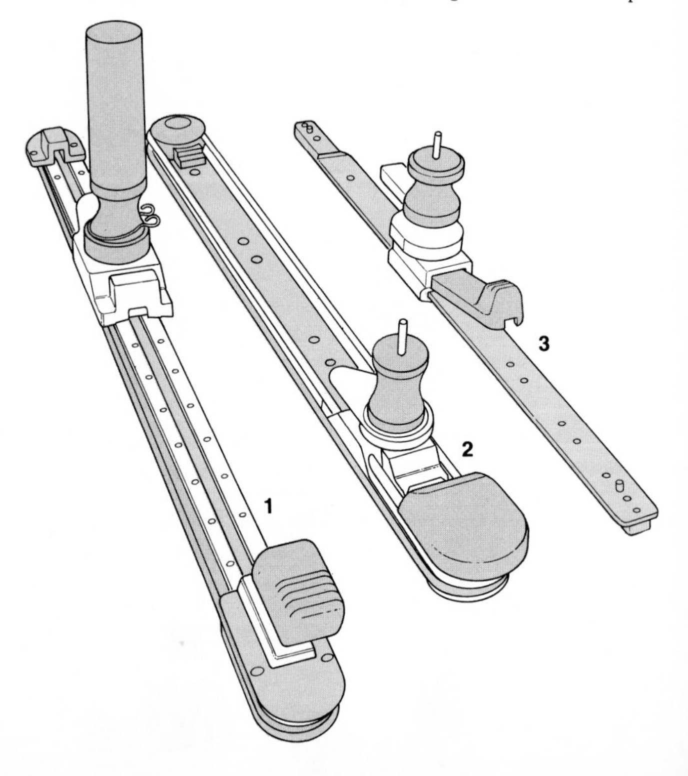

Mast tracks are available in a variety of lengths – the longer the board, the longer the track tends to be.

Most have a fixed foot pedal (1 and 2) mounted on the end of the track nearest to the daggerboard. However, in some cases this pedal can be mounted on the tail of the board where it can be depressed by your back foot.

Some tracks have a foot pedal which is mounted on the mastfoot and moves with it (3). This is a simpler and cheaper piece of engineering for the manufacturer, but likely to be difficult to operate in strong wind conditions.

One important consideration is the size and type of foot pedal. Big ones tend to be easiest to use, but are also easiest to set off accidentally. It depends on whether you sail barefoot or with boots.

that they seem destined to wear out after minimal use.

Short Board Tracks

It is less usual to have an adjustable track on short funboards. Without a daggerboard trim is more constant and, therefore, you should expect to set your mastfoot in the right position to suit the rig and conditions before you leave the beach.

On a very short board an adjustable track would be virtually useless as any attempt to work it would result in the board sinking, and the benefit would be barely noticeable.

Marginals

In the case of a marginal board of around 2.95 m, an adjustable track does aid upwind performance, provided that the mastfoot is moved to the front of the track to enable the whole length of the board to give lateral resistance upwind.

Care of the Track

Of all the equipment on a board, the track is the most likely to develop faults. Regular washing with fresh water will help to keep it running smoothly and, if it proves difficult to move, a shot of silicone spray will help it on its way. You must take care to keep the spray well clear of the deck of the board.

If the track seizes up completely, it should be easy to replace on a well-known brand of board. The track is usually a self-contained aluminium or plastic unit which is screwed into or on to the deck – the only snag is likely to be the expense!

You should also look at your track with your own safety in mind. Some tracks are really too dangerous for barefoot use, in which case you must always wear shoes or boots or get the track changed.

When the daggerboard is fully down and the mast track is fully forward the rig is in beating trim (below **A**).

When the daggerboard is fully retracted the CLR moves back and the mastfoot must be moved back (above) to put the board in good reaching trim (below **B**).

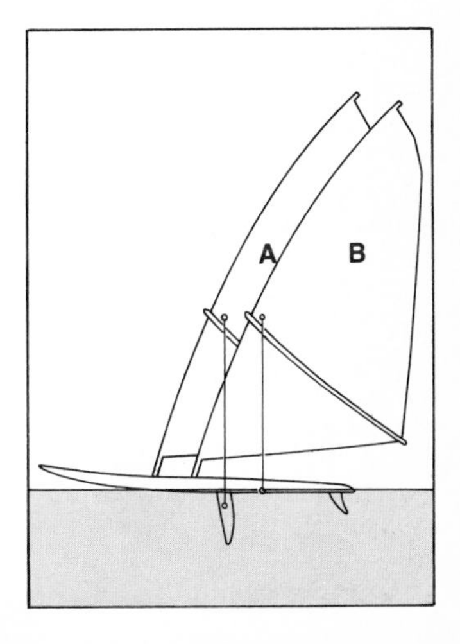

Mast Track Technique

1. Most adjustable track systems have a foot button at the back of the track. When rounding up from a reach to a beat, the first action is to push down the daggerboard (keep your back foot in the strap for stability). Then step on the mast track button.

2. Drop your arms in a sweeping arc down towards the nose of the board. This should make the mastfoot shoot to the front of the track.

3. If it doesn't want to budge, sheet it in to give the sail a little more power. This should be enough to pull it forward. Otherwise you should check for corrosion and maybe try a silicone lubricant.

4. When bearing off from a beat to a reach, the first action is to kick up the daggerboard so that it's fully retracted. The board soon picks up speed on the reach. That's the time to step on the mast track button – once again you should have your back foot in a strap to maintain your balance.

5. Lifting and pulling up and back in a sweeping arc should pull the mastfoot to the back of the track in one movement. Then you can step back into the reaching straps.

6. Most people find pulling the mastfoot back much more tricky than pushing it forward. In fact it's best done when you're moving fast on a reach because there's less apparent wind and it's easier to balance. If you try it when moving slowly you often get a bad wobble.

Both movements, backwards and forwards, should be practised on dry land so that you know what to do with your arms and body before trying it out on the water.

Sails

Fun sails vary in area from under 4 sq m to over 8 sq m. The size of sail needed by an individual in a given wind strength is almost impossible to define precisely, since the correct choice needs to take into account the user's skill, weight and athletic ability. Bear in mind too that sail-makers have different ways of measuring their sails, and

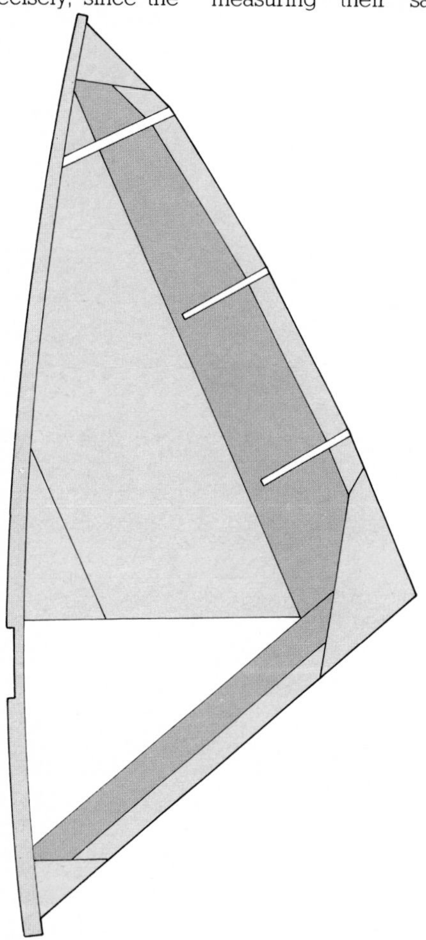

Vertical or radial cut sails have all but superseded the conventional horizontal cut. The vertical panels allow for different weights and types of cloth in the various stress areas of the sail, and as many as five different materials may be used in construction. If the seams radiate vertically from the track (the main point of tension in a sail) the sail is termed radial cut.

The change to vertical cut was partly made possible by the advent of Mylar, with its multi-directional stability. It also encouraged the development of the ultra high aspect sail which is fully-battened (much more stable in conditions with fast changing apparent wind speeds) and has a super-short wishbone with a high clew – sometimes the foot of the sail is battened as well.

Both sails shown are 4.6 sq m; the left-hand one needs a 4.5 m mast with a 2 m boom; and the other 5 m mast with a 1.45 m boom and is suitable for a much shorter board.

sometimes err on the side of exaggeration. A 5.5 from one sailmaker may turn out to be smaller than a 5.5 from another. Often the only way to check on exact sizes is to lay one sail on top of another.

Choosing Sail Sizes

Remember that experts usually opt for a sail which they can handle easily rather than a large one with which they have to struggle to maintain control. This is particularly true when sailing on waves which give added speed to the board and can have an enormous effect on the apparent wind.

The only exception is likely to be funboard course racing on flat water – the top sailors struggle on the upwind legs, with devastating results when they bear away on to the reaches.

Wishbones

The most important recent funboard development has been the move to shorter wishbones and high clews. The old standard wishbone which was designed for use with a 'regatta' sail is now obsolete. For general use, the maximum size sail is liable to be around 5.7 sq m (15 knots) coupled with a wishbone that's no longer than about 2 m.

Advantages

The short wishbone and high clew combination has four significant advantages:

1. Manoeuvring, either tacking or gybing, is much easier since the clew of the sail and the wishbone remain clear of the water.

2. Uphauling the rig requires much less effort.

3. When reaching in waves, the clew remains clear of the water.

A radial cut sail showing how tension radiates from the tack through the vertical seams. All the panels have varying weights so that the draught can be positioned accurately in the forward part of the sail. One hand is enough to control a good fun sail in manoeuvres.

4. The short wishbone sail has the Centre of Effort further forward which makes it less inclined to luff and much easier to handle.

Outline

Back in 1981 most sails designed for high winds were

pinheads with straight or concave leeches and no battens. These sails are quite satisfactory but they lack the ease of handling which characterizes sails which are partly or completely fully-battened.

Fullhead Sails
The 'fullhead' style has one or two full-length battens in the head to support extra area in the leech. This makes it possible to build a larger sail for a given wishbone length. The batten or battens encourage the upper part of the sail to twist open automatically in strong gusts, thereby both reducing the tendency to luff and making the sail more predictable and easier to handle in varying wind strengths with a stable Centre of Effort.

Fully-battened Sails
The fully-battened sail is a more recent development which, like most aspects of funboard design, originated in Hawaii. Fully-battened sails are designed for easy handling in exceptional winds by keeping the maximum camber forward, keeping the sail relatively flat, and retaining a high aspect sail plan with high clew and short boom.

Their main advantages are that the battens hold the sail in a constant flow shape in gusty conditions. This is particularly important for control of the rig when sailing at greatly differing speeds on waves. In addition, the leech support from the battens gives the designer freedom with his outline shape.

Fred Haywood introduced a brand new element into rig design when he broke the World Speed Record at Weymouth in 1983. However, commercial use of wing masts has proved impractical so far.

Shape, Cut and Fullness
The cross-sectional shape of a sail is a vital factor in determining its handling characteristics. For the majority of us a fun sail's most important feature is the ease with which it handles. The best way to achieve this is to make the sail with the maximum fullness fairly well forward, while ensuring that there is sufficient leech tension to keep power in stronger winds.

Flat Sail Design
A relatively flat sail is easier to

handle than a full one. Fullness and flatness are built into the design by shaping curved seams on each panel – making a luff curve to suit the mast bend (any extra in the luff will appear as fullness near the front of the sail) and, in the case of fully-battened sails, adjusting batten tension to tune the camber of the sail.

Vertical and Radial Cut

Most sailing craft use sails with conventional horizontally cut seams. This was standard for windsurfing sails as well until the advent of vertical and radial cut sails which are at present the norm for funboards.

Their great advantage is that cloth weights and types can be varied to suit specific areas of the sail. For instance, there may be heavy reinforcement on the leech, head and foot, with a more conventional material in the central, full area of the sail. Then a lighter material can be used in the low stress area next to the mast sleeve.

Sailcloth

Choice of sailcloth is a complex matter which has a fundamental effect on sail design and shape. Understanding its influence on sails is made doubly complicated by the variety of trade names and terms for materials which may be found on a funboard sail.

Polyester

Polyester (Dacron, Terylene etc) is the conventional sail-

Speed trials always bring out the most amazing sail designs. Unlike the Haywood 'Wing', few of them work – they are less efficient and more difficult to use than conventional sails.

cloth made by spinning plastic fibres into a yarn which is woven into a fabric and then heat treated. Characteristics of this material are determined by two factors – the weaving and the finishing.

The more dense the weave the more stable the cloth, given that the yarns are of adequate quality. However, cloth is very much affected by the finish, which ranges from a very firm, highly-resinated variety to cloth which is as soft as a dishcloth. It is important to realise that hardness does not necessarily confer stability and softness may not imply weakness. Some highly-resinated fabrics may lose their finish quickly and soon become very stretchy. On the other hand a well-finished soft cloth may have low stretch and retain that characteristic over a long period of time.

The most suitable material for recreational sails is generally considered to be a soft, well-finished material. As it gives a high degree of stretch on the bias, the sail shape can be controlled by downhaul and outhaul tension. The softer cloth is also more likely to suit a wider range of masts with varying flexibility.

Mylar

Less conventional are the shiny plastic film materials which are collectively known as Mylar. In fact, Mylar is the trade name of DuPont, Melinex of ICI and Teijin of a Japanese manufacturer licensed by DuPont.

Standard Mylar sailcloth consists of a thin polyester cloth (eg Terylene) – bonded to one side it's called single-ply; bonded to both sides it's two-ply.

The stretch characteristics of this composite cloth are determined by the film, while the tear strength is determined by the cloth. This combination results in a highly stable cloth which is considerably lighter than the conventional Terylene or Dacron.

Disadvantages of Mylar

Mylar does however have significant disadvantages:

1. It creases easily and great care must be taken when the

In recent years rigs have developed faster than boards. One of the big breakthroughs was the 'Wing' mast (left) used by Fred Haywood to break the World Speed Record in 1983. It was developed for use with sails by Neil Pryde. But rival sailmakers began to experiment with their own wings and there were promises of their appearance in production form. So far this has not happened – they are very difficult to tune or use correctly. Their cost would also be prohibitive since it requires sophisticated construction techniques to achieve very light weights.

Another advance was the development of pure Mylar sail fabric such as Airflex (right) which relies on a light nylon scrim in the middle for tear strength. It is lighter and less prone to delamination than Mylar/Dacron laminates.

sail is stored. Heavy creases will lead to delamination of the film.
2. The tear strength of Mylar is much lower than conventional sailcloth.
3. Mylar sails are very stable and allow for no error in the matching of luff curve to mast bend. Mylar sails normally require high quality masts which are very stiff.

Polyester Scrim

A recent development has been the Mylar scrim laminate (such as Airflex) – a two-ply Mylar sail in which the polyester cloth is replaced by a polyester scrim which looks like a fishing net and provides the necessary strength to prevent the Mylar from ripping.

The advantages are a cloth which is very stable, very light, simple to repair and completely see-through. The seams can be heat welded or glued, and while some sailmakers are using this material for their windows, others have adopted it for the main body of their sails with cloth reinforcment on the leech, foot and luff.

Just how short can a boom get? This one measures around 1.3 m, but is specifically designed for use in big Hawaiian surf where the sailors manoeuvre very close to the wave face and don't want the end of the boom digging into the water.

For more general use a boom of this length is too extreme. The rig will lack drive in flat water, and it's easy for the sailor to oversheet and fall off to windward.

High fashion should never be muddled with good design and practicality. This is eminently suitable for its intended use but not at all suitable for more ordinary funboard conditions.

Flaking and Rolling a Sail

1. A Mylar/Dacron laminate sail should always be rolled to avoid any creases which can leads to delamination.

However if you have storage problems you can 'flake' and roll it. Get someone to help you and start at the head, flaking it like a concertina along the luff and the leech.

2. Work down until you reach the foot of the sail. The width of the folded sail at this stage should correspond to the length of the sail bag in which you will store it.

3. Roll from the leech to the luff. You should take great care not to put hard creases into the window material which is prone to cracking.

Never store a sail like this when it is wet or has salt residue on it. Wash it down with fresh water and leave it to dry under tension. Letting it flap will soon destroy the finish.

Rigging and Sail Trim

A modern funboard rig is a highly-tuned piece of equipment. Great care needs to be taken if it is to perform correctly and stand up to the rigours of sailing in extreme conditions.

1. Start by laying the sail out on the ground. If it is fully battened, put the battens in at this stage. Allow them to protrude 45 cm from the leech so that the luff sleeve is straight and the mast can be accommodated. Slide the mast up the sleeve until it fits firmly into the tip of the sail.

2. Most sailmakers specify the necessary mast length. If it is over 4.5 m you will need an extra long mast or an extension, which should be slid into the base of the mast.

3. Slide the mastfoot assembly into the extension and make up the downhaul line. Only apply light tension to keep it all in position and remove the wrinkles from the luff sleeve.

4. For the conventional inhaul lashing, pass the wishbone over the sail and manoeuvre the jaws into the correct position. The height is critical and should correspond to your sailing style – about eye level is usually right.

5. Manufacturers invariably supply inhaul lines which are too short. It is important to be able to get several turns through the boom end and round the mast. Rotate the mast to and fro with your free hand to ensure that the inhaul line is pulled tight.

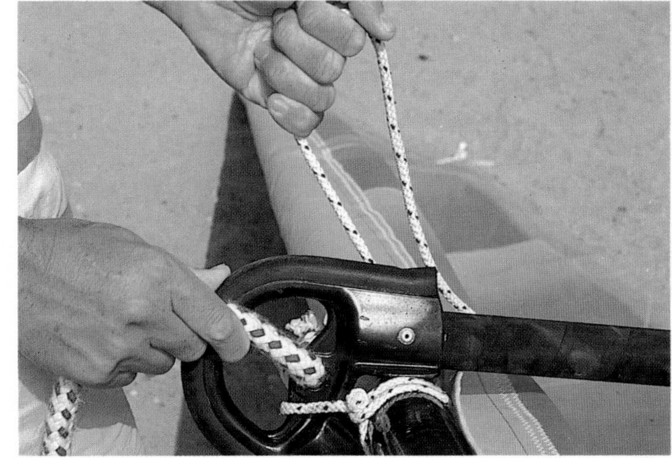

6. A cleat is normally provided but the inhaul line can just as easily be secured with two half-hitches round the wishbone. There is sometimes an annoying free end which is left flapping about. It's not a bad idea to use a rubber band to hold it in place on the boom.

The inhaul must be very tight, with the boom held absolutely rigid against the mast.

7. Slide in and secure any short battens before making up the outhaul. The inner end of the batten normally locks on to elastic inside the batten pocket. The outer end of the batten slips into a fold in the cloth on the leech.

8. Arrange a 4–1 purchase on the outhaul. Pull until the sail goes flat along the wishbone and then fasten. At this point the sail will still look full above and below the wishbone as the final downhaul tension still has to be applied.

9. Push the full-length battens fully home until they locate at the inner end of the pocket by the mast sleeve. The outboard ends should protrude by about 2.5 cm.

10. All fully-battened sails have some sort of tensioning buckle at the end of each batten. The batten should be tensioned until the pocket is taut and free of any wrinkles. Sail camber can be tuned in this way with batten tension.

11. Return to the downhaul. Again use a 4–1 purchase and pull hard. This is very important as it brings the fullness to the front of the sail and makes it balance.

12. The sail should look flat with a small ridge of fullness immediately behind the mast sleeve – if this doesn't appear, pull harder on the downhaul until it does. If the ridge is too big and the sail too full, pull harder on the outhaul.

The wishbone must be rigid and at the right height. If the inhaul line fails to grip the mast when you pull on the uphaul (usually with an alloy mast) you should wind tape around the mast in the appropriate position.

Rigging Tips

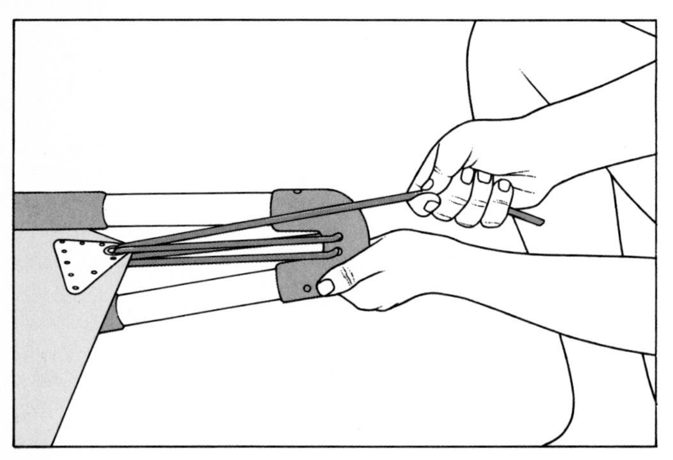

Outhaul
The simplest and best outhaul only requires a short line. Pass it through the wishbone end, secured by a stopper knot. Take it through the cringle in the clew, back through the pulley or hole in the boom end, and secure it in the single cleat which is within easy reach. If the sail has a clew handle, it's easy to tension the outhaul with one hand on the handle and the other pulling the line through the cleat.

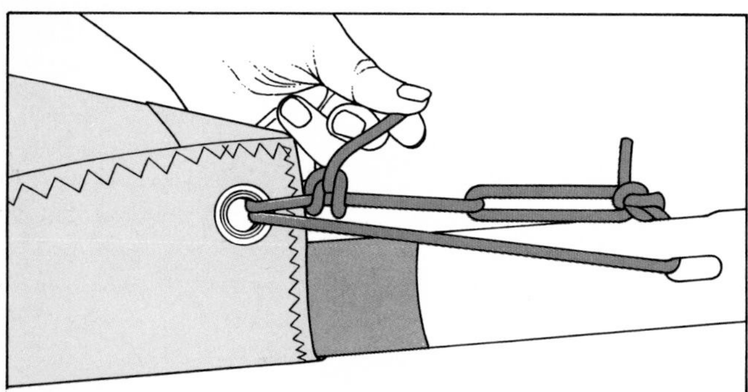

Downhaul
The downhaul needs at least a 4–1 purchase. Pulleys and a tack handle help. Or you can run the downhaul through the loop of a bowline and back through the cringle for maximum purchase. To adjust the downhaul, brace your feet against the mastfoot base and pull.

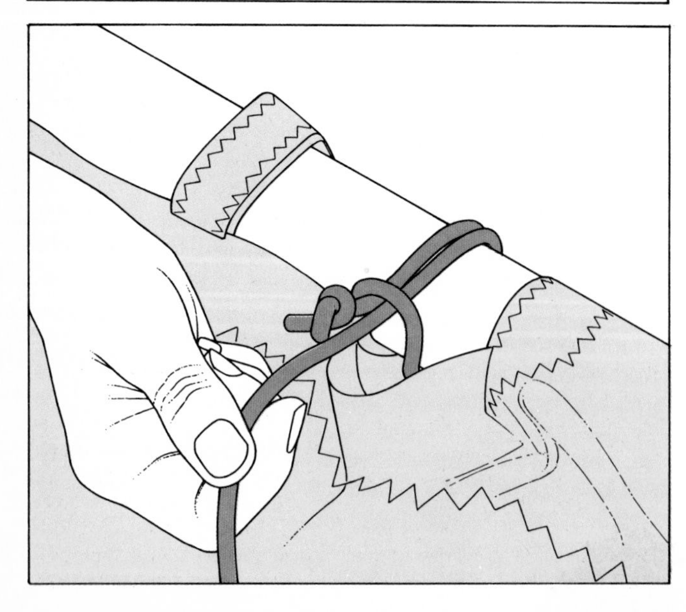

Inhaul
The simplest inhaul may slip. If it does you can try tape on the mast, or an alternative lashing such as the rolling hitch which locks tight but is difficult to undo or adjust.

Depending on the boom end fitting, there are a variety of ways of fixing the boom tightly to the mast. The system shown on pages 52–53 is based on the excellent Mistral boom end fitting and can be adapted for different designs. Other makes (North, Klepper, Fanatic etc) are equally effective but work on entirely different principles – most of them are sold with instruction leaflets!

Sail Trim

All masts bend, and the luff curve and camber in a sail has to be cut to suit that bend. If the sail is not suitable for the mast you will get a poor set, even though both sail and mast may be excellent products in their own right.

Most production sails have a compromise cut which is designed to be suitable for a wide range of masts that are generally available and fitted to most of the mainstream production boards.

The fancier high performance sails, however, generally have more specific requirements. If you are willing to pay these high prices you should also be given information on the right masts. Exel, Serfiac, Ampro and North are some of the best known names for stiffness and high performance.

You can see straight away if the mast is wrong for the sail. When it's all set up there will be creases running diagonally upward from the clew which indicate luff starvation – usually this means that the mast is too soft (poorer quality) for the sail, and you will have to change to one that is stiffer.

Racers require super stiff masts and booms for high performance. But the recreational sailor should bear in mind that a stiff rig may be unforgiving and difficult to use, even though it is efficient. For enjoyment, a little flexibility in the rig goes a long way to making funboard sailing easier.

If mast and sail are compatible, the most important aspect of sail trim is the downhaul. Modern funboard sails are designed for an enormous amount of downhaul tension, and it's a common mistake to have too little. Remember also that a new downhaul line may stretch, so you will have to keep re-tensioning it to keep the sail in trim.

With fully-battened sails, the batten tension is also critical. Too little, and you will see wrinkles along the batten pockets.

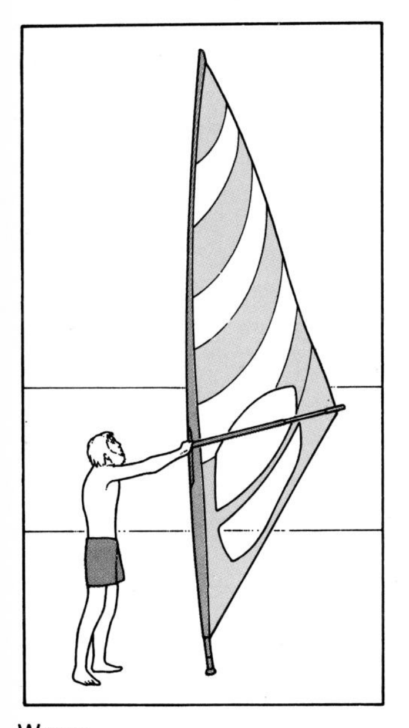

Wrong
Too little downhaul leads to horizontal creases, most prominently along the luff and the mast tube. The solution is to apply as much downhaul tension as necessary until the creases disappear.

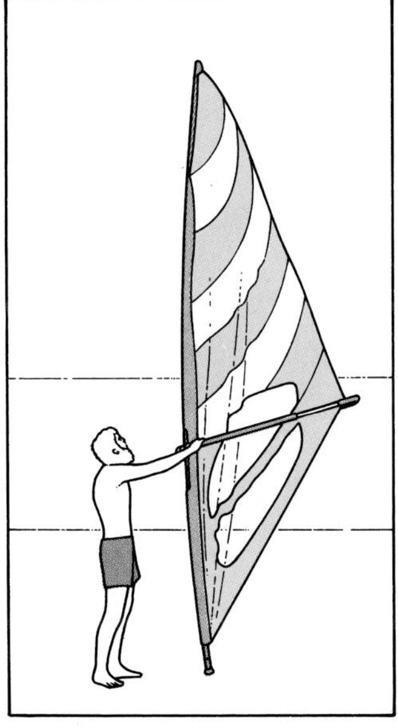

Wrong
Vertical creases signify too little outhaul tension, so the solution is to pull harder on the outhaul. In some cases there may be too much tension (either outhaul or downhaul) causing the creases which should be slacked off.

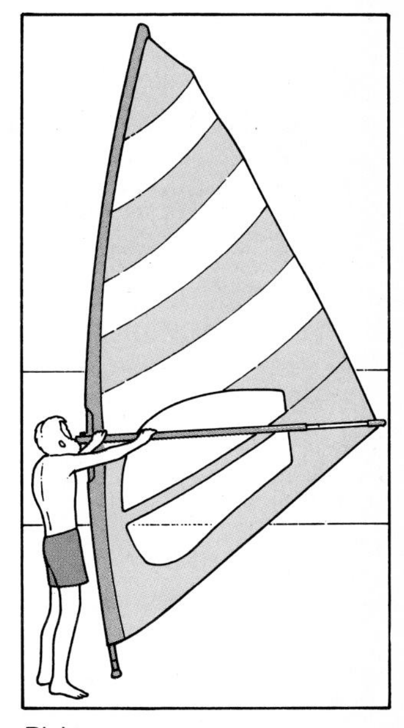

Right
A nicely trimmed sail. The correct amount of tension on downhaul, outhaul and the full length battens. The mast is a fair match for the sail and its luff curve though there are faint signs of luff starvation indicating a soft mast.

Preparation

Weather

The Wind

As long as there is enough wind (constant and from Force 4 upwards) the funboard sailor doesn't need to worry. However, it certainly helps if the wind is accompanied by some sun and warm water.

Wind is created by two means – differences in atmospheric pressure and the effects of the sun heating up the land and sea.

Highs and Lows

When atmospheric pressure is high (called a High or anticyclone) the weather tends to be settled and good. When it is low (a Low or depression) the weather tends to be bad.

The wind blows from areas of high pressure towards the low pressure areas. Wind strength is dictated by the amount of difference in pressure in the two areas. Pressure is measured in millibars on a barometer and shown in isobars (two millibars) on charts.

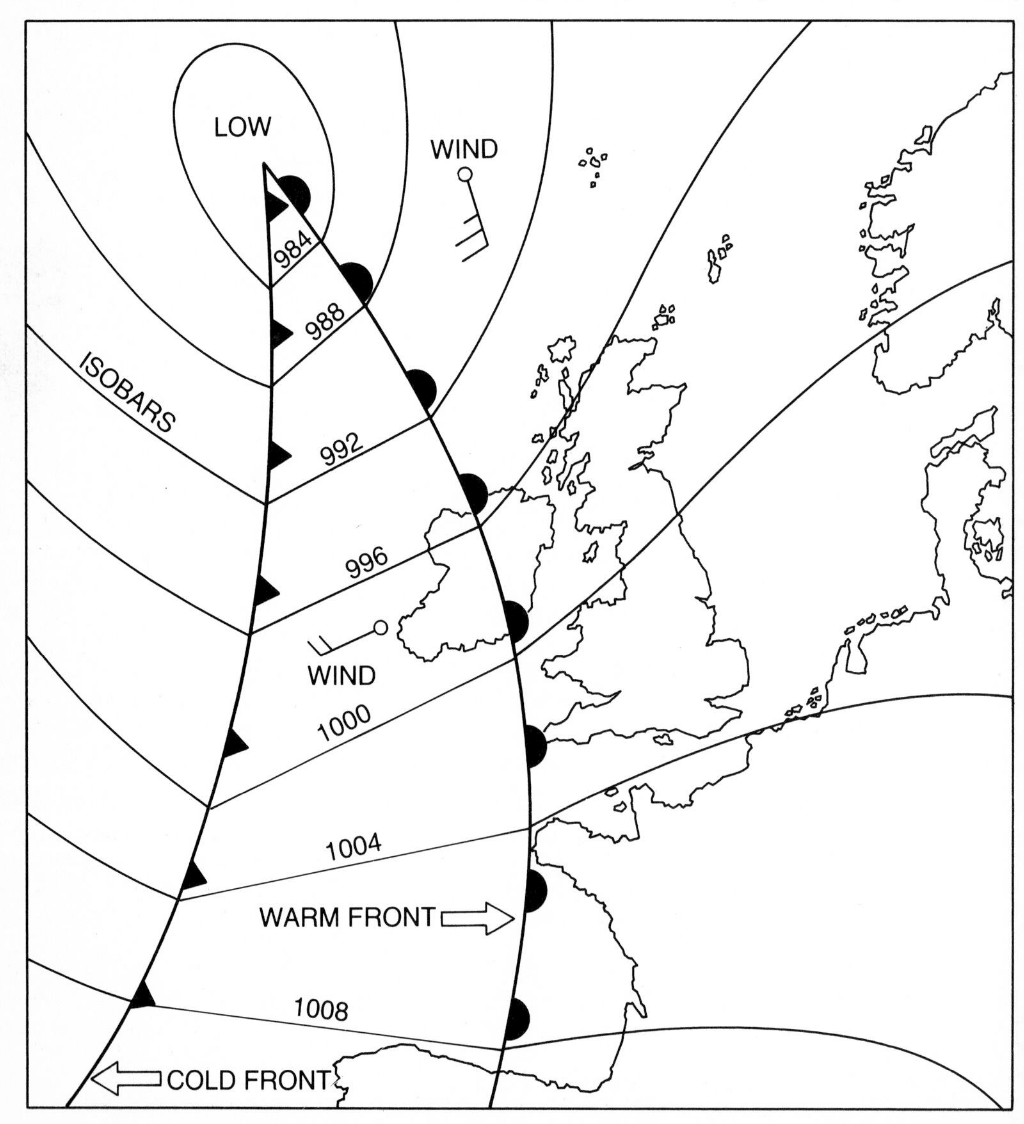

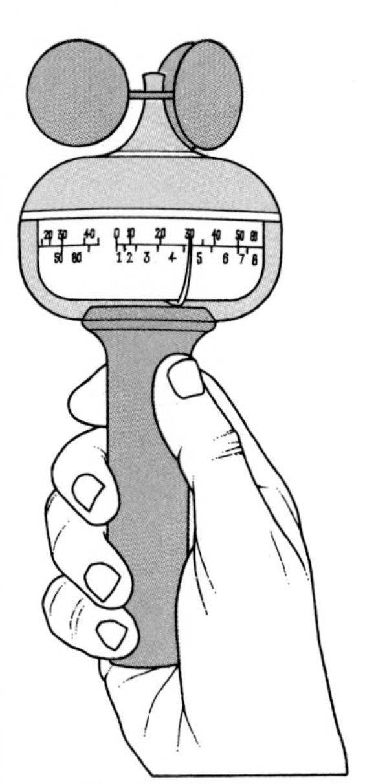

Above: Hand-held anemometers allow you to read the wind off a scale which may be marked in knots, miles per hour, kilometres per hour or sometimes in the Beaufort Scale.

Left: A typical weather map for the UK. Wind direction follows the line of the isobars. The closer the lines, the stronger the wind. 'Fronts' mark the boundaries on the surface between air masses of differing temperature. A 'warm front' marks the boundary on the surface between a mass of advancing warm air and the cooler air over which it rises. In a 'cold front' the advancing cold air acts as a wedge to push up the hot air. Wind shifts are likely to occur at fronts, particularly cold fronts.

Sun and Sea

Every morning the sun heats up the land more quickly than it heats the sea. Hot air starts to rise from the land, creating a low pressure area which draws the much cooler air from the sea towards it. An onshore breeze is created, building in strength as the sun rises. Once temperatures drop as the sun begins to set, the land cools more quickly than the sea and the process is reversed. A low pressure area develops over the water (now warmer than the land), draws the cool air and creates a slight offshore breeze.

Exceptions

There are many exceptions and variations in the effects of Highs and Lows and sun and sea:

Trade winds

The Trades are steady Force 4+ winds which blow from the high pressure Horse Latitudes (see wind map on page 122) and create the winds for the most famous windsurfing areas of the world – Western Australia, the Hawaiian islands, the Caribbean, West Africa, the Canaries, etc.

Monsoons

Monsoons are winds caused by the sun and sea effect on a large area of land, even a whole continent.

The best example is the Indian monsoon which blows onshore in summer (south-east) and offshore in winter (north-east).

Drainage winds

The influence of sea and sun on the wind can be exaggerated or altered in mountainous regions. When the land cools, cold air sinks into the valleys which act as a funnel and accentuate the wind's force, creating particularly strong winds which blast down towards the water.

This type of wind is common on Lake Garda in Italy and in the Mediterranean, where the high, cold mountains create winds such as the Mistral. This funnels down the Rhone valley to the French Mediterranean coast.

The Scirocco is a different type of hot drainage wind. It is caused by low pressure over the western Mediterranean which draws hot air from the Sahara.

Forecasting

There are some rules of thumb which are useful if you wish to do your own weather forecasts or interpret weather maps like the one shown on the left.

1. Wind increases during the day and dies at night.

2. Wind is more likely to increase if it is sunny and/or blows obliquely along a coastline which causes it to funnel and gain speed. If it is cloudy you won't get the benefit of a sea breeze.

3. Surface winds and the winds indicated by the lines of the isobars may have as much as thirty degrees difference in direction.

4. A well-established High may not give way to a Low. If the Low is coming from the west, you should go west to look for the wind.

5. A Low does not necessarily mean plenty of wind. The centre of a Low is just as calm as the centre of a High, but rainy and cloudy, and with no thermal influence.

The Beach Start

With a sideshore wind the neatest way to launch a long funboard is the beach start.

If the board is light enough to pick up, a much smarter and easier launching technique is shown on pages 64–65.

Like so many aspects of windsurfing, the beach start originated on Kailua Beach in Hawaii. This beach has soft sand, a constant sideshore wind and only a small beach break. That makes it easy to launch a board. But, if the wind is more onshore, or if a shelving beach creates dumpers to crash down on the board, it is often very difficult.

You may also have to contend with shingle or a concrete slip. You will need to decide how much you value your board and how tough its skin is. Harsh surfaces may cause serious harm.

Technique

The technique for the beach start is always the same. With the board pointing out towards the water, line up the rig so that the mast is on the correct windward side of the board with the clew downwind.

Lifting the Rig

You can then pick up the tail of the board with your back hand (usually there's a handy footstrap). At the same time lift the rig, so that the wind can blow under it, by placing your hand on the mast just above the

This is the style of allround funboard (Mistral Maui) best suited to the beach start. It's much too big to carry, but has a tough ABS skin which is impervious to being slid over soft sand.

1. The rig must be in the right position for starting. If it is not, either flip the clew or walk the rig round until it is properly aligned. You can then pick up the tail and the rig, and slide it down into the water.

2. Once in the water the board will usually show a tendency to round up into the wind. Any waves will exacerbate this as they push the nose to one side or the other. If a beach start seems impossible you must carry the board into the water (a short board is easier). Then drop it on to the surface and jump on very quickly so that you can sail off before the waves wash you back up the beach.

wishbone cut-out.

Using the Rail
If the board sticks in the sand, flip it up on edge so that it can be slid along on its rail. This is much less likely to cause damage to the skin on a rough surface and the board should be much easier to slide.

Push the board into the water until it's deep enough for the skeg to be clear of the bottom when you climb on the board. Transfer both hands to the wishbone, and line up the board for a beam reach by pushing (or pulling) on the mastfoot.

The daggerboard must be fully retracted and, waves permitting, the board should then turn about its skeg.

When you're at the right angle, test the wind in the rig. If there's a little pull it makes it much easier to get up and off. Step up with your back foot. Then, while sheeting in and raking the rig forward, bring up your front foot and sail away.

Beach Return
Returning to the beach you must reverse the process. You hop off before the skeg grounds and grab the back strap while holding on to the mast with the other hand. Slide the board as quickly as you can up the beach. When the nose is clear of the water walk the tail round through 180 degrees into the wind.

3. A fully retracted daggerboard allows the sailor to align the board for a beam reach. He just pushes or pulls with the wishbone (the effort is transferred to the mastfoot) and the board turns about its skeg.

Once everything is right, you can hop on. Look out for the tail sinking which will cause the board to round up into the wind. Avoid this by raking the rig forward, sheeting in, and weighting the outer rail.

4. In light wind you can't rely on the rig pulling you up on to the board. It doesn't matter if conditions are calm, but with any waves an unstable board and lack of support in the rig can make the beach start difficult. Remember to step into the middle of the board with your weight over the mastfoot when starting in light wind conditions.

Retrieval

1. Coming ashore on a moderate length allround-funboard you can reverse the procedure for the beach start for a really neat landing.

As you come in towards the shore on a reach (sideshore wind) slow down by pushing the sail forward so that the rig has a braking effect. Keep the board going straight, and hop off before the skeg grounds, keeping both hands on the wishbone.

2. Keep the board straight by pushing on the mastfoot and reach for the backstrap with your back hand. If there are waves and the board is being pushed about, you have to do this quickly, while keeping the rig clear of the surf.

Speed is important, as a vicious shorebreak can make short work of a mast.

3. Keep the board straight and slide it up on to the beach. If necessary you can flip it on edge if that makes it easier.

As soon as the nose is on dry land, start walking the tail of the board in a 180 degree turn into the wind. Keep a loose hand on the rig to support the boom, the mast or the uphaul rope.

4. You can walk the board round in a couple of seconds. The rig will begin to flip as it passes through the eye of the wind. Take care not to make the mistake of turning the board away from the wind. This can lead to the rig being forced down on your head as the wind gets on the wrong side of the sail.

5. This is the point where the sailor lets the rig flip over on to the new tack. He continues turning the board until it is lined up for another beach start, walking it backwards to get away from the surf or the incoming tide.

6. The end of a very slick landing which gets a chorus of approval from onlookers on the beach. For an even smoother landing you need a short board which is light enough to be plucked bodily from the water and carried ashore. See overleaf for techniques of carrying boards in and out of the surf.

Getting off the Beach

Carrying a Short Board
Because it's small and light, you can pick up and carry a short board with its rig. This is generally a good idea since short boards tend to be made of more fragile materials, and don't take kindly to being pushed or dragged down a beach.

The easiest way to carry it all is to grab the nearside front strap, put your head under the window, hold the mast just below the boom and lift. Just be careful that the wind doesn't take control – keep the rig flat and low with the clew flying free downwind.

Launching and Getting Out
It's best if you can carry the board through the beach break and drop it when you reach the slightly flatter water beyond. Then you can hop on and take off as shown in the photo sequence.

When you come back in, the process is reversed. Slow the board and hop off before the skeg grounds. Grab the nearside front strap, get your head under the window and a hand on the mast. Then lift it up and hurry ashore before the waves take control.

Sideshore Wind

If the wind is sideshore, get your feet in the straps and just blast out through any waves or white water.

If the wind's more onshore, getting off the beach will be less simple. On a beam reach the waves will strike the windward rail of the board from nose to tail. A breaking wave will wash the board back into the shore, depowering the rig so that you fall in to windward. It's a time when an instant waterstart comes in useful.

To avoid this problem, the best technique is to head the board up straight towards the oncoming white water. Then lift the windward rail which will help guide the board cleanly up and over the wave.

Offshore Wind

If the wind is more offshore, there will be a substantial reduction in the apparent wind as board and rig are travelling in a similar direction. The sailor will rely heavily on the board for directional control, and with little drive the rig will tend to feel mushy and unresponsive.

An offshore wind is also liable to be gusty but it will tend to flatten the waves. You can choose to sail out on a diagonal course on a close reach to get some power in your rig. Remember to lift the leeward rail as it will hit the wave first. This will direct the board up and over, rather than into the wave. As the board will be thrust shoreward and into the wind – increasing power in the sail dramatically – depress the windward rail and lean back immediately.

Basic Technique

Uphauling

Uphauling in funboard conditions can lead to the most violent case of wobbles. Frequently the rig gets dropped back into the water as you lose your balance. You also get progressively more tired as you uphaul again and again.

1. The correct technique makes uphauling much simpler. Start by pulling up the rig with a straight back and comfortable stance. Then lay a hand on the mast when it comes near enough to reach.

2. Let go of the uphaul rope and pull the clew clear of the water to get the power out of the sail. Quickly pull the mast over towards you and into the wind. Use your free arm to keep balanced.

3. Bring the mast across in front of your nose and spin on the balls of your feet to face forwards, looking through the window. Note that the front foot is behind the mastfoot throughout the sequence.

Next, reach out for the boom with your back hand.

4. The windier it is, the more the rig should be inclined to windward. This will combat any tendency the board has to head up into the wind.

5. Drop your front hand on to the boom. Then pull in evenly on the rig, leaning back if necessary to take the power in the sail. If the board shows any tendency to round up towards the wind, push like mad with your front foot – if necessary move it down on to the edge of the rail. Remember to keep the rig forward, and use the power in the sail to force the nose of the board away from the wind.

6. Uphauling and getting under way in moderate winds is quite easy. In rougher conditions it's another story – strength sapping and sometimes impossible. If you are to succeed you need total commitment and quick, decisive movements, but in that sort of wind it's generally quicker and easier to perform a waterstart. See pages 86–93.

Beating

Beating technique is important to get you back upwind, particularly when sailing in tidal conditions.

Long Boards

When you change from a reach to a beat, step forward with your front foot to push down the dagger. Keep your back foot in the back strap.

Use the rig for balance and step on the mast track button. Sweep your arms downwards and forwards to shoot the mastfoot to the front of the track (see pages 42–43).

Beating Stance

Then take up a beating stance. Very few boards are fitted with proper beating straps, so the best bet is to wedge your back foot in the back front reaching strap, and perch your front foot on the rail about level with the end of the mast track. Lean your body forwards and twist it so you can look straight ahead as you sail along.

You may get problems with railing. The answer is to push down with your front foot and/ or sheet out a little. A lot depends on your technique, but if railing persists, try retracting the dagger until you can control it. You can let the leeward rail dig in a little for extra lateral resistance. It will also help prevent your front foot from getting washed off the side of the board.

Short Boards

The short board relies on speed to get you home. You have to keep it planing while going close upwind, digging in the windward rail so that you use the whole length of the rail like one long daggerboard.

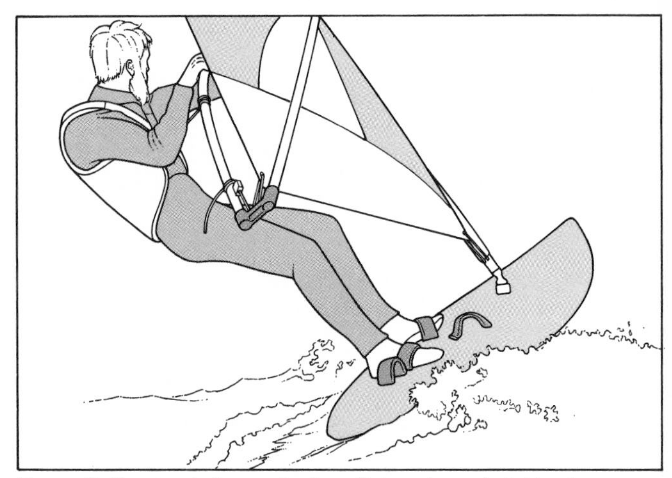

Above: Sailing upwind on a short board, your legs should be close together with the body leaning forward and with the windward rail buried.

Below: A comfortable stance on a long board. The mast track allows the rig to be held fairly upright while the body leans forward.

Reaching

Funboards are made for reaching. They should never sail on a run (too slow and unstable) and beating should be kept to a minimum as it is simply a necessary evil.

Long Boards
When bearing off from a beat you initiate the turn away from the wind by allowing the leeward rail to bury itself at the tail. Meanwhile your body is lifted upright by the rig.

Move forward to kick up the dagger. Then step on to the mast track bottom, keeping your back foot tucked into its strap to help preserve your balance. Lifting and pulling back with a sweep of your arms should pull the foot to the back of the track in one movement – it helps if you are already travelling fast on the reach.

For a comfortable reaching stance your back foot should be in one of the back straps and your front foot in one of the front reaching straps.

Close Reach
If it is a close reach you will be going quite slowly, and the chances are you will use the front set of straps. If you're really moving fast on a broad reach, you may need to get right into the back set to keep the tail in contact with the water. At the same time you should keep a little pressure on the leeward rail to help prevent spin-out.

For maximum speed, keep the rig as upright as possible!

Short Boards
Few short boards have adjustable tracks. If they do, pulling the mastfoot back increases power by bringing the rig into a more upright position, and increases manoeuvrability by getting the foot close to the skegs (CE close to the CLR).

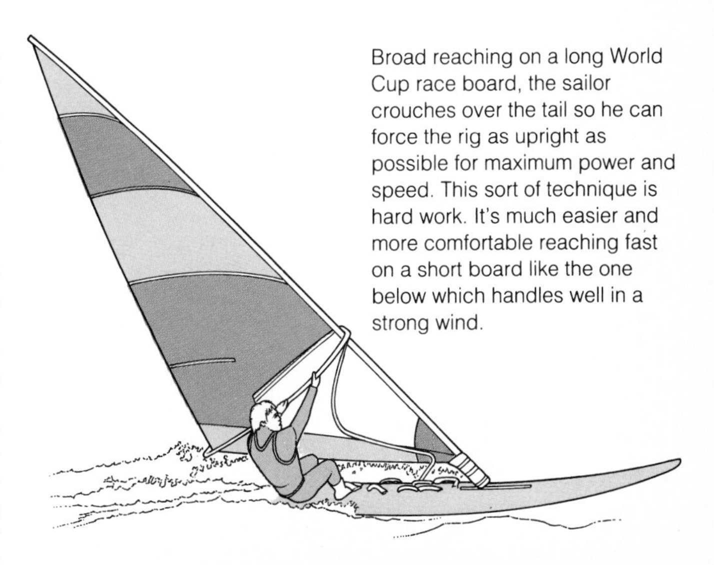

Broad reaching on a long World Cup race board, the sailor crouches over the tail so he can force the rig as upright as possible for maximum power and speed. This sort of technique is hard work. It's much easier and more comfortable reaching fast on a short board like the one below which handles well in a strong wind.

Spin-out
You can detect spin-out as soon as it starts. The tail of the board begins to slide away from you as the skeg ceases to grip. You can control this by sheeting out, losing speed and digging the lee rail into the water. Then wait until the skegs grips the water once again.

If spin-outs seem completely uncontrollable, try standing further forward to take the weight off the tail.

Tacking

1. Tacking a longer funboard can be difficult. If it has a mast track, the foot will be at the front of the track – it means you have a long way to step round the front of the mast, and there is likely to be very little area or volume in the nose to step on which is why gybing is easier.

2. If you're racing, keep tacks to a minimum – with a big skeg, the board will turn slowly and the chances of a fall are high. When the moment comes, rake the rig back and pull the clew round sharply into the wind, leaning back to push on the tail and make the board head up.

3. As the nose passes through the eye of the wind, take a long step forward to get your foot braced against the front of the mastfoot. Drop your front hand on to the mast, let go the boom with your back hand and keep your weight inboard.

4. Step forward with your back foot, and stand in front of the mastfoot holding the mast with both hands. If the track is a long way forward the board may become very unstable, particularly if there are any waves.

5. Step round on to the new side, rake the rig forward with your mast hand, and reach out to grab the wishbone with the other hand. If the nose sinks, be prepared to move your weight back on to the middle of the board, and power the rig to make it bear away.

6. Getting the board to bear away requires aggression and speed. Lean right back, powering the rig with your sheet hand and pushing the nose of the board away from the wind with your front foot pushing against the side of the board or the mastfoot with the rig raked forward.

7. A conventional allround-funboard with volume and stability forward of the mastfoot should be relatively easy to tack in moderate wind conditions. If you have problems getting round the front of the mast, try sailing with the mastfoot pulled further back in the track. This simply gives you more room on the nose of the board. If the conditions are really wild, you'll invariably find that it's easier to gybe, though more ground is lost to leeward as you make a much wider arc.

Footsteering

As soon as the wind picks up to around 12 knots, an allround-funboard has enough dynamic lift to plane. You can 'footsteer' it like a waterski without needing to rake the rig back and forth to head up or bear away. You can steer more quickly and simply with your feet.

Obviously conditions and the type of board are important. A minimal sinker travelling at 20 knots will footsteer much more quickly than an allround-funboard travelling at 15 knots, but for both boards the principles and technique remain the same.

The daggerboard must be fully retracted with the board planing on a beam reach. You can hook in and hang on comfortably with your feet in the straps and your weight taken by the rig.

You can steer a slalom course without moving the rig. Just pull and press on the rails using your feet in the straps and the board will alter course. If you press on the leeward rail, burying it at the tail, it banks the board like a ski and make it bear away. Thrusting your knees forward is enough to do this. All the pressure goes on to the rail.

To turn back towards the wind you must put pressure on ('weight') the windward rail at the tail. Do this by straightening and stretching your front leg, while the toes on your back foot help to lift the rail. The rig remains in the same position all the time so that you continue to plane and get maximum benefit from the wind.

Any allround-funboard worth its name should be able to footsteer when it's planing, though it may seem sluggish and need a fair amount of effort for steeply banked turns. Sometimes little tricks, such as pumping the rig to pick up speed on small waves, will help it along.

The sequence on these pages shows the basic technique for footsteering a long board:

1. Plane along on a reach with your feet in the straps and your weight taken by the rig.

2. To bear away thrust your knees into the turn. This has the effect of weighting the leeward rail.

3. The board banks like a waterski and bears away from the wind without any need to move the rig.

4. To head up, straighten your front leg and pull up on the leeward rail with your back foot so that the windward rail is weighted at the tail. The board immediately heads up (**5** and **6**).

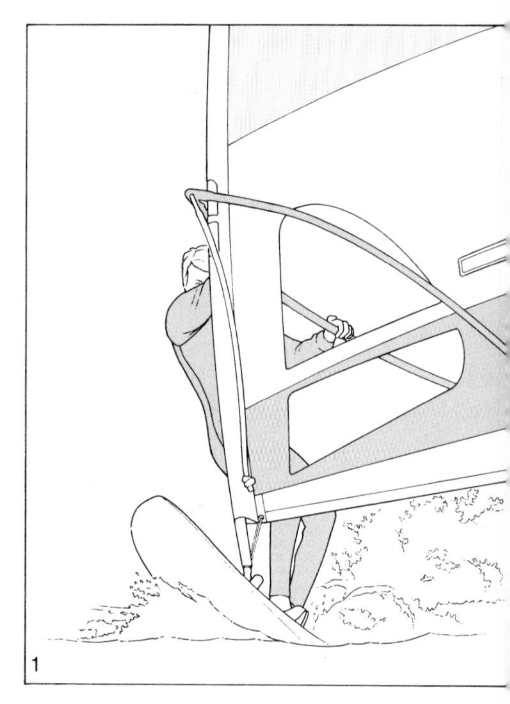
1

4

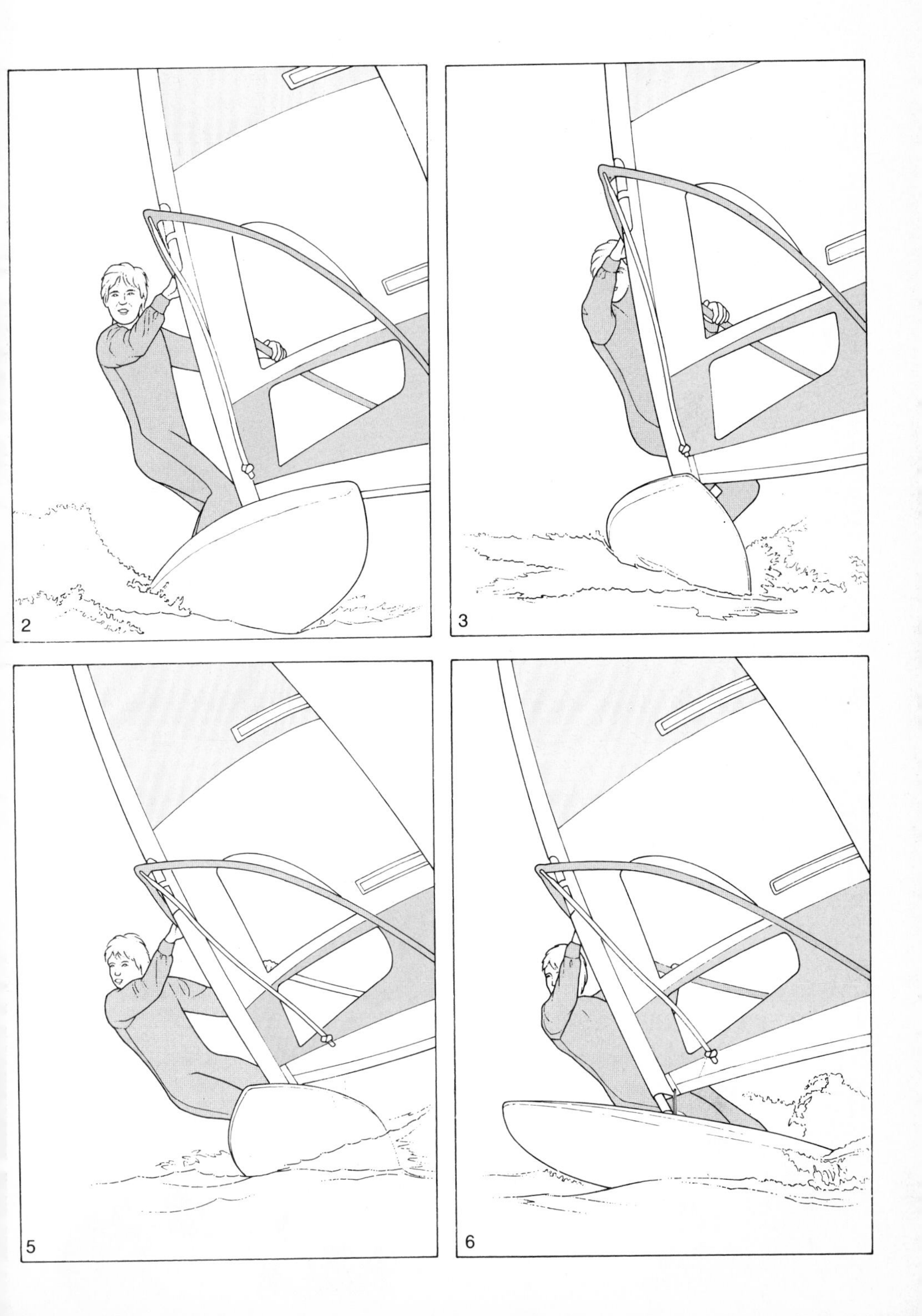
2
3
5
6

Carve Gybes

Funboards carve gybes, and the technique is quite different from the conventional style of gybing.

Forget about raking the rig and sinking the windward rail to make the board turn (a flare gybe). If you're sailing a funboard and planing fast, a gybe is initiated by pulling up on the front strap and sinking the leeward rail by the tail. This will bank the board into a turn away from the wind. The turn is continued smoothly and at a maximum speed until the board has carved through 180 degrees – from broad reach to broad reach. You can then flip the rig and sail off on the new tack.

The Right Board

To carve gybes you must have the right board and the right conditions. The main requirements are speed, a low volume pintail profile (with rails that grip the water and determine the arc of the gybe) and footstraps to control banking the board.

Try the following test while sailing at full speed on a reach. Lift your front foot in the strap and press down the leeward rail with your back foot:

Excellent response throws you and your board into a sweeping curve away from the wind. Only a short board (under three metres) is likely to perform like this.

Average response, and the board bears away gradually without requiring any movements from the rig apart from sheeting in.

Poor response, and the rail submerges while the board continues in a straight line without bearing away.

Gybing a long board

Its length makes carves on a long board difficult. Speed must be maintained, the daggerboard must be fully retracted and the arc of the gybe will have to be wide.

If the board drops off the plane during the gybe, you will need to resort to powering the rig clew-first to continue sailing the board round. If that fails, you can change to a flare gybe.

Gybing a Short Board

Carving a short board at slow speeds is hard, and requires more balance than at high speeds. For preference you should be out in Force 4–5, making around 20 knots.

Bear away smoothly by lifting with your front foot in the strap. Ease down on the back foot which should be taken out and placed just in front and a little over the centreline from the back strap.

Don't crank the back of the board in. This would stop acceleration (a 'slam gybe' – used to pivot the board in a short arc during slalom racing). Just ease into the turn smoothly, keeping the sail tuned to the wind, and concentrate on maximum speed.

Your body should lean 60% in and 40% backwards. The 60% inward lean turns the board while the 40% reduces the waterline and makes the board turn easily. Don't lean in too far – the rail may dig and make a straight edge with the result that the board just goes in a straight line.

Another big problem for beginners occurs when the board bears away and shoots off downwind losing a lot of ground. Once on the run the sail becomes difficult to control and pulls you off balance. This frequently results in the beginner pushing down on the wrong rail. The solution to this is to leave the rig in its upright sailing position rather than leaning it into the turn (this can come later). Use its power to help you footsteer the board round, ease the rail in, get the board biting, and then ease in more to carve a smooth arc.

Don't step too far back on the tail which may stall the board. If you feel any loss of speed move your weight forward. Think of your sinker like a railway engine – it requires little effort to maintain speed once it's moving, but if it stalls or stops it's extremely hard to get started again.

Once the board is biting and you are leaning into the turn, you are committed. Don't falter – see it through and avoid jerky movements.

Remember that a gybe is a progressive manoeuvre and not a stop/start sequence.

Complete the turn and let the rig flip round. If you can get this far without moving your feet, your gybes will be 100% better. After taking out your back foot, the last thing you want to do during a gybe is change the position of your feet. You should start sailing on the new tack with your feet in the old position so your body has to twist in to face the sail. It is then easy to pivot on the ball of your back foot and slide your front foot across into the new front strap.

The only way to achieve good gybes is by constant practice – the sequences (right) show you how its done.

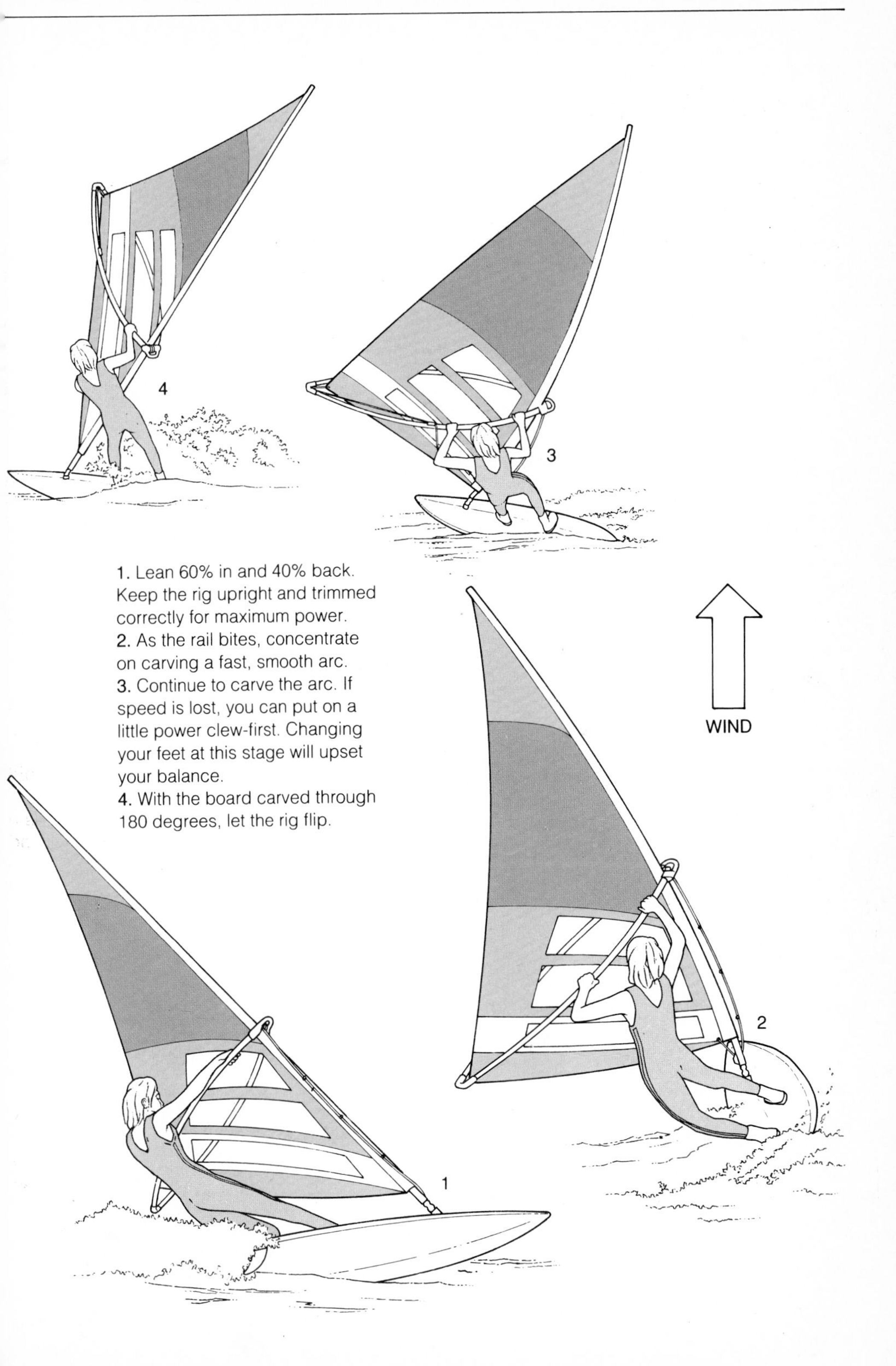

1. Lean 60% in and 40% back. Keep the rig upright and trimmed correctly for maximum power.
2. As the rail bites, concentrate on carving a fast, smooth arc.
3. Continue to carve the arc. If speed is lost, you can put on a little power clew-first. Changing your feet at this stage will upset your balance.
4. With the board carved through 180 degrees, let the rig flip.

Gybing a Long Board

You should be able to carve gybe on any of the allround-funboards. The main requisites are a fully retracted daggerboard, a low volume tail with hard rails that bite the water and plenty of wind so that you're travelling at full bore on a reach.

The faster you go, the easier it is to gybe. Due to its length, a long board should only be carved in a wide arc to keep it planing throughout the turn. If you start to lose power you should sail clew-first to keep the board moving through the turn. If it drops off the plane you will have to hop back on the tail and sink the windward (outer) rail for a flare gybe.

1. Start the turn with the mastfoot right back in the track.

2. Take your back foot out of the strap, place it near the leeward rail by the tail, lift with your front foot and thrust your knees forward and into the turn.

Remember to keep the rig upright and correctly trimmed so that you keep the power on all the time.

3. The board banks and goes into a turn away from the wind. It's quite easy to control the arc of the carve, which will depend on how much you bank the board. When you're rounding a racing mark like this, come in from outside and take it in a wide sweep to keep the board planing. The limiting factor will be if other boards are gybing round the same mark and cramping your gybe area.

4. Keeping the board on the plane with the rig working takes the board through the eye of the wind and on to the new tack, ready for the sailor to gybe.

This is the point where a lot of sailors run into problems. They gybe too slowly or too tight and don't keep power in the rig so the board loses momentum. The apparent wind increases and as pressure grows in the rig, the board shoots off on a dead run. The longer the board, the more it naturally tends to stop the carve and straighten out.

To prevent this and continue the carve, you can power the sail clew-first. If that doesn't work and you stop planing, you'll have to resort to a flare gybe.

The One-handed Gybe

The one-handed gybe is a fancy refinement of the conventional carve gybe – it's basically doing something a little different that looks good from the beach.

Everything should happen in the few seconds when your board speed (think of 20 knots) comes close to matching the wind speed. If that was 25 knots, there would only be five knots of wind in the sail.

When you move your hand forward, either catch hold of the mast (or to the boom very close to the mast) so that the sail can pivot easily while you concentrate on manoeuvring your body and the board.

'Feel' the board as you ease it into the turn. You must do this firmly but gradually so as not to stall, and once started you are totally committed.

The first time you trail your hand try crouching. Then, as you gain confidence you can start to straighten your legs. You will find that leaning in so far turns the board very quickly. As you approach the end of the turn push down with your front foot to shift your weight a little forward – you don't want the tail to drag and reduce the waterline as the board might drop off the plane.

This also has the effect of straightening out the board. As you get both hands back on the boom you should resume full power immediately before changing feet.

1

4

1 Bear away at maximum speed and take your foot out of the back strap. Wait for the sail to go weightless as your board speed comes close to matching the wind speed.

2 Move your front hand to the mast so that the sail can pivot round freely.

3 Lean gradually into the turn and a little backwards, to get the rail to bite the water.

4 Once it bites, dig the rail in hard and let your hand trail in the water.

5 Quickly go straight back to the boom with your hand, and start to level the board out.

6 Sheet in to put the power back on and help pull yourself up. Leave moving your feet until you have completed the gybe.

3

6

The Duck Gybe

The duck gybe is, naturally, a Hawaiian invention which was first tried and demonstrated by Richard Whyte.

It's not as quick or efficient as the conventional carve gybe (you never see it used in a competition slalom), but it looks much more fluid and is an established part of the wavesailing and general showing off windsurfers' repertoire.

There are many variations on how you can do it. The easiest method is described here, while a slightly different technique is shown opposite.

Technique

The duck gybe is initiated just like the regular carve gybe. Go at maximum speed, take your foot out of the back strap, and ease into the turn.

While bearing away, slide your rear hand as far back as comfortable – the further the better: a high clew, short boom sail makes life easy.

As you feel the board start to bite, ease in more. The sail will begin to feel lighter as the board's speed matches the wind. At that point release your front hand and cross it over your back hand, again as far back as you can. If you time it right the mast won't suddenly fall away as there is so little wind pressure in the rig. If it falls away near the water, you can do it better next time.

When your hands have crossed, you can let go with what used to be the back hand, and pass it under the foot of the sail to grab the boom as you pull the rig quickly over your head with the other hand.

Common Mistakes

For an instant you hold both booms, and during this time it is imperative that you hold a steady carve. People often forget what to do with their feet (you should be good enough at the standard gybe to carve the board without thinking) and let the board straighten out and sail downwind. The speed drops and the apparent wind increases, so that while you're doing five knots there may be 20 knots in the sail – it's obviously difficult to catch or control it.

The Right Way

Back to the right way. When you grab the new boom your front hand must be as far forward as possible. This makes it easier to sheet in on the new tack, or to spill wind if there's a gust when you're about to catch the boom with your second hand.

With both hands on the new boom, sheet in and power the board through the final stages of the gybe. Sail out of the turn on full power before changing your feet.

This is the easiest way to duck gybe though some prefer to use the foot of the sail.

Duck Gybe using the Foot of the Sail

1 Reach at maximum speed and start the carve.
2 Now start one of the many duck gybe variations. Slide your rear hand back, and when the rig goes light, let go with the front hand and grab the foot of the sail.
3 Let go with the back hand and sweep the foot of the sail across your body.
4 Catch the new boom with your new front hand, followed by the new back hand. Put the power on to complete the gybe.

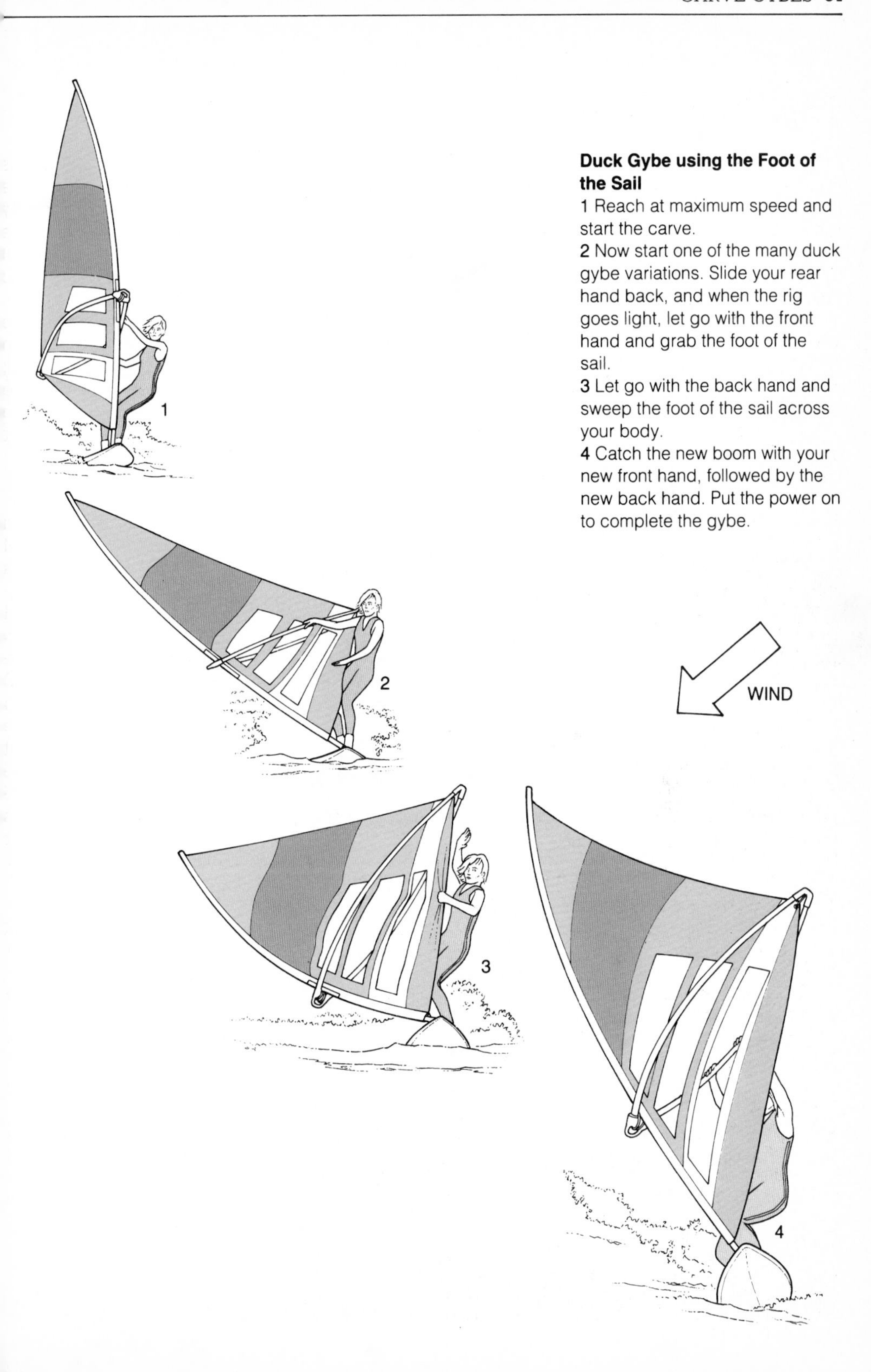

The One-handed Duck Gybe

This is a combination of the one-handed carve gybe and the duck gybe. It should not be tried until you have mastered the other two.

Timing is much more critical, and more speed going into the turn (and throughout it) helps a lot. The difference comes when you remove your back hand. Instead of going straight for the other boom, let your arm fall free and drag your hand in the water. This turns the board faster, and loses speed. A frequent mistake is to hold your hand in the water for too long. The board goes all the way round and, before you know it, the rig backwinds on top of you. While dragging your hand it's imperative to 'feel' the board and be aware of your position in relation to the wind.

After dragging your hand, it's essential that you grab the boom as near to the mast as possible. This allows the sail to spill wind when you release the other hand.

With experience you will find it much easier to catch the boom if you gybe from close reach to close reach, so that the boom only needs to go out a few inches to spill wind.

1

1. Go at maximum speed and initiate a duck gybe, but do all the movements faster.

2. Crouch slightly while changing over hands. Instead of grabbing the other boom, lean in further and get the board biting.

3. Get your body comfortable and lean in more so that you can trail your hand in the water.

4. You will find the board turns much faster.

5. Quickly take your hand up to the new boom and continue, getting both hands on the boom, as in a regular duck gybe.

6. Put the power on and bring the board round through the final stage of the turn – you will find that the board comes out further round than usual, due to the extra leaning. Finally, move your feet to the right position.

4

3

6

The 360

Here's how to 'unwind'. You should already be an excellent short board sailor and a master of the various gybes. You need fairly flat water, an easily handled rig, a short boom and a board no longer than 2.7 m.

1. You must be going very fast or you will never get the board through the 360.

2. Get the leeward tail biting and lean forward on to the rig.

3. This is the point of maximum speed when the rig goes weightless as board speed and true wind are matched on a downwind course. Lean on the rig and start holding it down so it's just clear of the water.

4. By now you should have gybed. If you have initiated a perfect carve the board will continue to carve round with the mast tip pointing into the wind and the whole sail feathered.

5. Things get difficult as the board slows up and there's a danger of the sail getting backwinded. This would flip it up and push you off the board. To avoid this it's imperative to keep a clear picture of the true and apparent wind direction, keeping the sail feathered and raked back over the tail of the board.

6. Almost there. This is the point where a wide tail and a little volume in the middle of the board may be important to keep it moving.

7. That's it! Even if the board has ceased its carve, the sailor can push on the mastfoot with his front foot and bring the rig upright to power and pump it to get the board to bear away.

8. Bearing away and picking up speed. Almost time to relax.

9. Back on the beam reach – congratulations, you've turned through 360°!

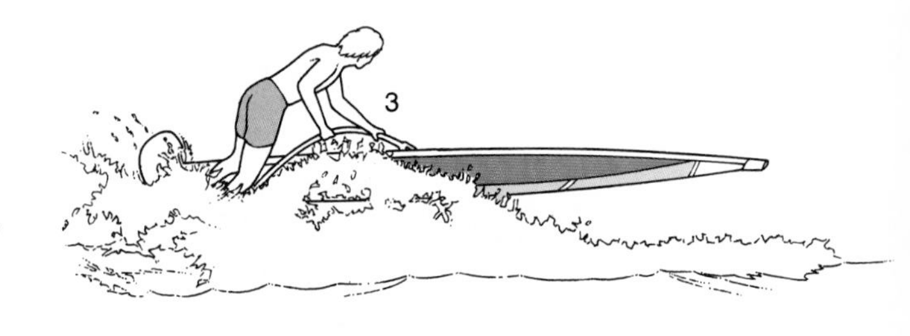

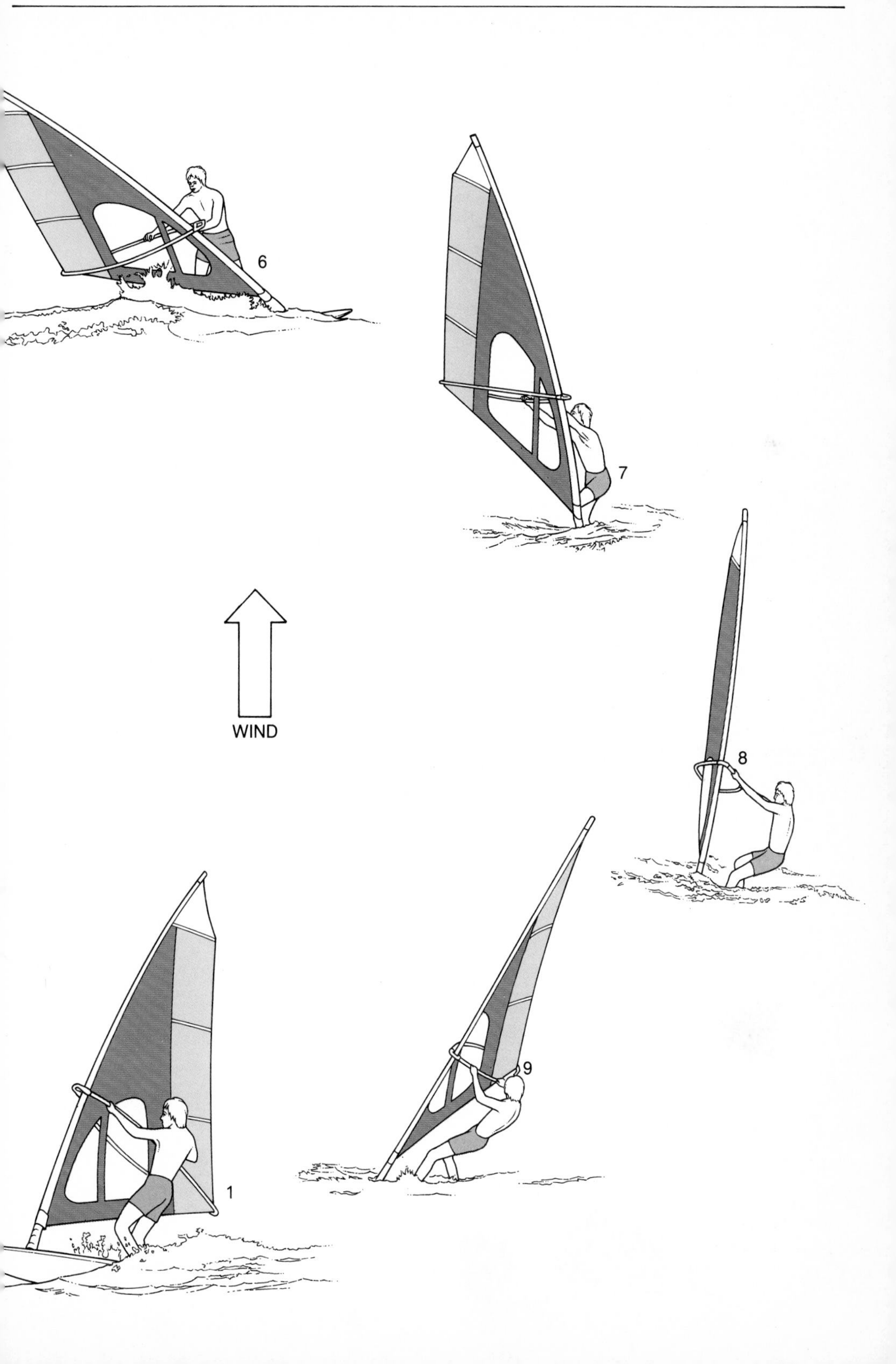
6
7
WIND
8
9
1

Waterstarts

Why Waterstart?

The waterstart is the most important technique in funboard sailing. Once you have mastered it you can handle virtually any board if the conditions are right. If you don't learn to handle it, you will be extremely limited in the types of board you can sail and in the conditions in which you can go windsurfing.

It's not a new technique. In the 1970's it was a regular feature of the freestyle event at Windsurfer Class World Championships. However, it only really came into its own with the advent of the short funboard, and in particular the sinker – the kind of board which cannot be uphauled.

In 1980 the waterstart was considered a fancy and difficult technique being used only by a handful of Hawaiian hot-shots. However, by 1984 it was being considered an everyday technique for all reasonably able sailors.

Pretty soon you can be sure it will be on the curriculum of any novice taking the first steps in learning to windsurf.

Less Strength Needed

Apart from unlocking the door to short boards and high winds, the waterstart has the advantage of being much easier and less strength-sapping than conventional uphauling. All you have to do is master the skills needed.

Requirements

The first requirement is the right conditions. You need a steady wind of about 12–15 knots. Any less wind and there will be too little power to pull you out of the water. More, and you won't be able to handle it.

Flat Water

The water needs to be relatively flat since waves pose an added complication. It must also be fairly warm since you will need to be prepared to spend a lot of time in or under the water. For this reason learning in a cold climate is extremely hard. There is always a good excuse to give up, clamber back on the board and revert to the old uphauling method.

Waterstarting technique is simple, but it does require waiting for the right amount of wind to pull you up and out of the water. This is difficult in light winds.

You should take a trip to the West Indies or Hawaii where being in the water is a pleasure instead of a torment! A couple of days with the right wind should be enough for you to master the waterstart.

Equipment

The second requirement is the right gear. A short board isn't necessarily bad since it will be much easier to manoeuvre when you're down in the water. However, it must be stable, it must float and it must support you when you are pulled up out of the water.

To a large extent the size and shape of the board must depend on your own size. A small, light person can learn on a small, short board. While someone carrying more weight will need a proportionally bigger board.

A rig with a short boom and high clew is a must for learning.

High Buoyancy Harness

Finally, it is a great help to have a high buoyancy harness which will keep you afloat while the rig is trying to push you down. It will also save you swallowing a lot of water (you'll still swallow enough). Make sure, though, that the harness doesn't ride up round your shoulders. You need a tight fit with four straps under the rib cage. Some harnesses are also fitted with crotch straps to keep them in the correct position.

Three-Part Sequence

A waterstart comes in three parts and requires three different techniques which need to be learnt separately:

1. Getting the board and rig in the right position.

2. Getting the rig up out of the water.

3. Getting yourself up out of the water and on to the board.

Clew-first Waterstart

This is an example of a fancy technique. It shows the ease with which the top guys can waterstart in an instant and from any position.

It's quite usual to fall off at the point when you start riding clew-first in a gybe. As you fall back in the water the situation can be remedied by keeping power in the rig, and waterstarting clew-first from the windward side of the board. As the rig pulls you up complete the gybe and sail on your way with just a few seconds delay but plus quite a few bonus points from among the spectators.

Waterstarting clew-first is handy if you fall off in the middle of a gybe. However it is very difficult with a long boom and regatta size sail – the shorter the boom, the easier a waterstart will be.

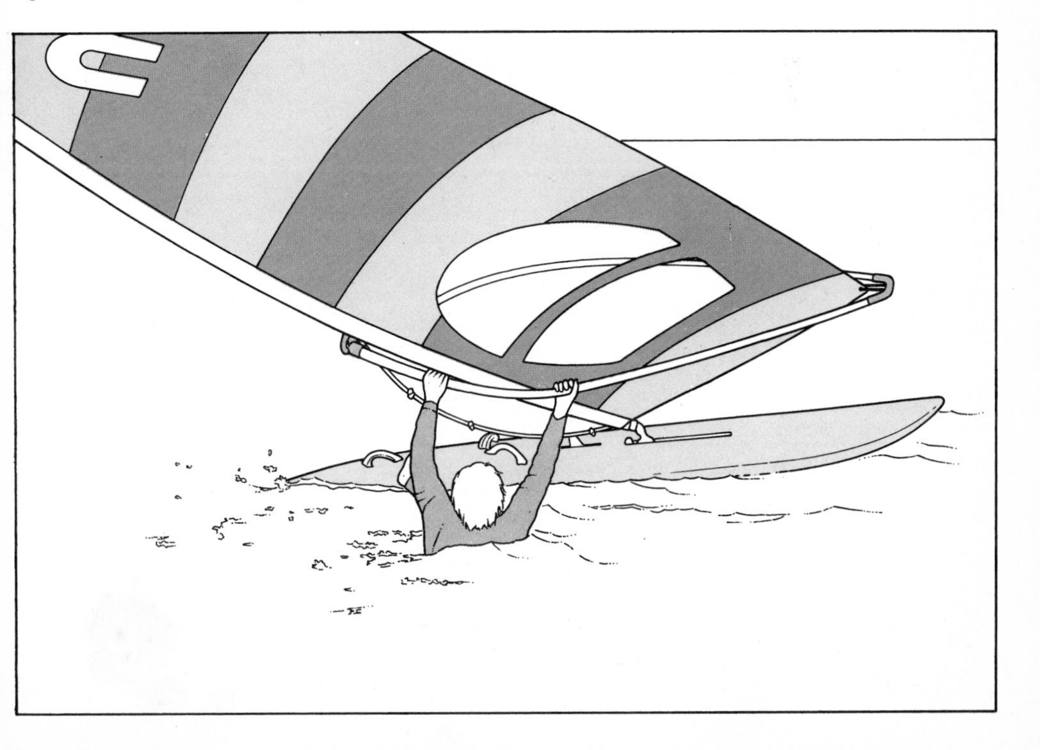

Waterstarts – Rig Position

The correct position for a waterstart is for the board to be pointing in the direction in which you want to go. The rig should be lying to windward with the wishbone end by the board's tail (ie the place where it ought to be).

However, when you fall in, either the board or rig (or both) is invariably in the wrong position. You have to work out the easiest way to get it in the right place. This either means flipping the rig, swimming the

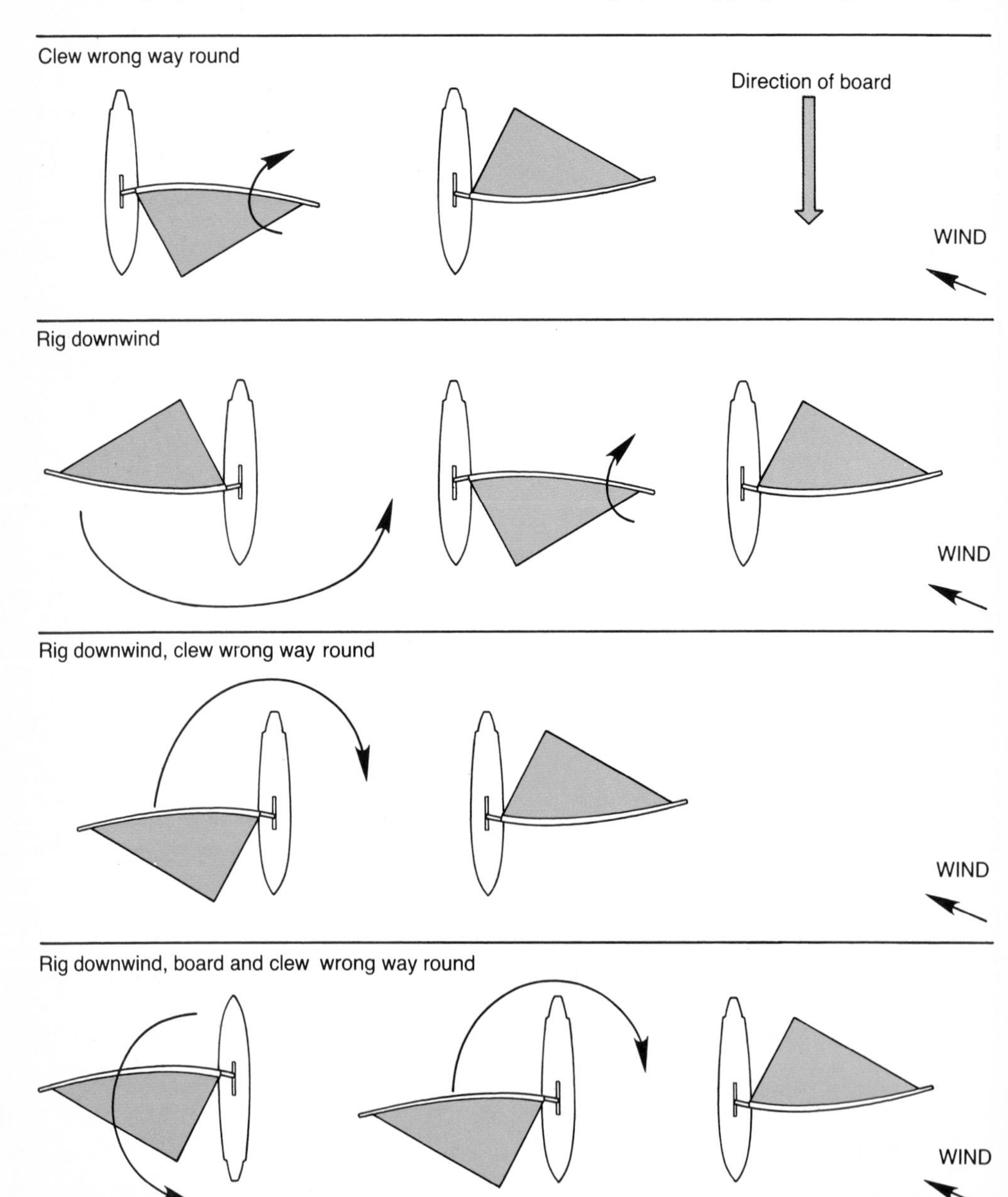

rig and/or swimming the board round, you can choose which you prefer.

Clew Upwind
If the clew is the wrong way round (by the nose rather than the tail), swim to it, lift it a short way clear of the water, then let the wind catch it and flip it over into the correct position for waterstarting.

Rig Downwind
If the rig is downwind, you must swim it round until it's on the right side of the board.

To do this, swim round and grab hold of the mast just above the boom. If possible lift the mast a little way clear of the water, and then swim it round to the correct side of the board.

Always swim the rig into the wind, leading with the mast. With the rig on the correct side, you can then swim to the clew, and lift it until the wind catches it and flips the rig into the right position.

Swimming the rig round takes time. With a short board it may be quicker to turn the board, and start in the other direction.

Rig Downwind, Clew Upwind
The sequence is much the same. You swim round to the rig, grab the mast, and swim it round to the correct side of the board.

Rig Downwind, Board and Clew Wrong Way Round
If you're on a short board it's easy to turn it the right way round. With relatively little volume the nose (or tail) can be pushed beneath the rig. You then get the rig into the right position by taking hold of the mast and, as before, swimming it round the board.

Lifting the Rig
For a learner it's usually easiest to swim to the top of the mast (above right) and lift it clear of the surface, holding it up like a sea anchor while the board blows directly downwind.

The wind blows along the mast, and it's easy to work your way towards the boom, supporting the rig with your front hand holding the mast and your back hand under the sail. The wind will provide adequate lift.

By the time you reach the boom it should have popped clear of the water, but if the clew is submerged swim the rig forward and into the wind until it pops clear. Then grab the boom with your back hand and give the rig a little power.

When you get better, it's quicker and easier to start off with the rig at right angles and the board facing directly into the wind (below right) – ie the wind is blowing straight along the boom. Grab the mast just above the boom and quickly jerk it up and forward over your head while swimming yourself forward. The quick motion should be enough to pop it clear.

Waterstarts

1. The rig is to leeward with the clew upwind. The sailor lifts the boom end fitting so that the wind begins to get under the clew. As the wind catches, he pushes the boom end higher.

2. He lets go and the wind flips the rig so that the clew is in the correct downwind position necessary to commence the waterstart.

3. Holding the tail of the board with one hand, he grabs the mast just above the boom. With a swift movement he pulls it across and over his head. This has the effect of accelerating wind under the sail and breaking the clew clear of the water. It also gets the rig over on the windward side of the board as he swims it forward into the wind.

. In the right position for starting
n a beam reach, he moves his
ack hand on to the boom
ollowed by his front hand.
heeting in with the back hand
ust a little) is enough to bring
he rig more upright and pull him
n closer to the board. Then he
an get his back foot up on to the
oard and into the forward back
ootstrap.

5. With his back foot on the
oard he can rest with his arms
utstretched. It's easy to get into
his position if there's sufficient
vind. If the wind is light, he
vould need to drop his front
and on to the mast (about
alfway between the boom and
oot) and bring his body close in
o the board to get the rig as
pright as possible.

6. The final stage of the
vaterstart is getting up and
way. He bends his back leg to
get in close to the board with the
ig upright. The additional
ressure in the sail tends to pull
he board sideways rather than
ulling him up, so it's important
hat he trails his front leg like a
sea anchor. As the rig begins to
ull him clear he kicks with this
eg until he can step up on to the
oard and swing his body in over
he centreline.

Waterstart – Sinker

1. Waterstarting a short board has problems and advantages. The problems come when the sailor steps up on the board – the tail is likely to sink under his weight, which must be transferred quickly on to the mastfoot. The advantage in waterstarting with a short board is that it is much easier to manoeuvre in the water, particularly if it (or the rig) is facing the wrong way.

One hand lifts the mast and the sailor swims the rig forward into the wind until the clew breaks clear of the water.

2. The sailor transfers both hands to the boom, sheeting in to power the rig and bring him forward and in closer to the board. Great care has to be taken not to overpower the rig with the sheet hand. The result would be that the wind takes control, tears the rig from your grasp, and you have to start all over again with the rig on the wrong side of the board.

3. With his hands on the boom, the sailor can manoeuvre the board into the right position for a beam reach waterstart. If the board is pointing too much downwind, raking the rig back will make it point more upwind. If it is pointing too much upwind, he must rake or swim the rig forward before the wind catches it on the wrong side and pushes him down in the water.

4. With the board in the right position he sheets in, stretches his arms and lets the rig pull him in close to the board. He can get his foot up on to the deck with his front leg hanging down and acting as a sea anchor, watching and waiting for the gust which will pull him free. When it comes he bends his back knee, making the board bear away as he pulls the tail towards him ready to bring his body in under the boom.

5. Note how his body looks as if it's going head first up the inside of the wishbone. He must bring his body in close over the centreline of the board so that he can get the rig as upright as possible with his weight supported by the high volume middle section of the board.

6. Even though it's not moving, the board will still respond to footsteering. If the tail sinks and the board begins to head up, the sailor should lean forward with his weight on the mastfoot and sink the leeward rail.

In some cases it may be easier to waterstart front foot first. It's all a matter of personal preference and technique, taking into account the board being sailed and the prevailing conditions.

Wave Riding and Jumping

Wave Jumps

The anatomy of a wave jump is fairly simple. If you're going fast on a bicycle and hit a bump in the road you will take off. The same thing happens with a funboard at speed and the wave acts as a ramp.

However there are tricks to ensure better, longer and more controlled flights. These are clearly shown in this photo sequence of a wave jump made off the island of Guernsey.

1. You want to hit the wave at maximum speed and as square-on as possible, choosing a relatively flat section for distance and safety – if necessary luff at the last second. As the board shoots up the ramp, lean back to get the nose going up and power the rig.

2. When you're in the air, tucking and crouching of the body will extend the glide of the jump. Lifting the windward side of the board will help to get the wind under it and give you more lift. But it will also blow you more downwind. You can counteract this by luffing the sail. Conversely, trimming the sail will prevent the board from luffing up into the wind.

. By this stage you should have
nought out your landing and how
o avoid the spin-out which so
equently follows. When you land
ne nose must be pointing
ownwind from the tail. To get
ne board angled correctly,
tretch your front leg (which
ushes away the nose) and kick
our back foot up under your
ackside to pull the tail towards
ou.

. A not so happy landing. If
ou're inexperienced, coming
own nose first can lead to a
asty wipe-out. Easiest landings
re made tail first (not flat, which
ould break the board and give
our legs a nasty jar) with the
indward rail leading the way,
ut not flipped right up on its
dge as is shown in this picture.
lowever, a tail-first landing will
tall the board. For experienced
ailors, therefore, it's better to
ome down nose first as this will
elp regain planing speed
nmediately on landing. Always
rouch over the centre of the
oard to maximize control and
ushion the initial shock of
anding.

Upside Down

With a strong wind, a short board and a steep wave you can invert the board for an upside down or 'table top' jump. The rig tip will just touch the water. You should aim for the steepest part of the wave at maximum speed, leaning back over the tail and pulling in on the rig to power the sail as the nose clears the lip. Then lean even further back and pull up on your front foot as the board leaves the wave.

As soon as the tail comes clear you have to kick the board up over your head and into the wind. Once it's up there you will start to drop, so you must smartly kick the tail back down to get it under you for a tail first landing. The nose should be downwind and you will be hanging from the boom. Don't leave getting the board back under you too long, or you will land on your back with possible dire results. If this looks like happening, be ready to bale out and kick the board away from you to ensure that it doesn't land on top of you.

Eric Thième, (below and right) emerged as France's waveriding star during the World Cup season of 1983. This sequence shows part of his competition routine during the San Francisco regatta which was eventually won by Peter Cabrinha.

A short light board and a high aspect sail with a short boom are essential for these fancier manoeuvres:

1. Thième heads for the steepest part of the wave. Timing is critical as the steepest section will be the next to break and crumble. He must hit it in the second before this happens.

2. With his weight over the back of the board he takes off while giving the sail full power. He kicks the board up over his head. Note that the tail is kicked into the wind (coming from the right-hand side of the picture) with the nose downwind. This is necessary for him to maintain control during the flight and get the tail down for a good landing.

At this point the tip of the rig is just brushing the water.

3. He pulls the tail of the board back down under him, but has left it just a little too late. The result is a painful landing on his backside, followed by a total wipe-out. It just goes to show that any of the fancier, more difficult wave manoeuvres demand the most precise timing if they are to be successful and injury is always a possibility.

1

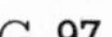

Chop Jumping

With speed and technique you can chop jump on wind-blown wavelets that are only a few cm high – alternatively the wake of a speedboat or power cruiser will be enough to get you airborne.

The requirements are a light, short board which planes easily and has a good take off area. The wide base of a diamond tail or swallowtail will get you up in the air much more easily than a drawn-out pintail. The other necessity is a powerful sail with high cut clew.

Hit maximum speed on a reach with both feet firmly in the footstraps (**1**). If possible you should be in the back set to take the weight off the front of the board and help lift the tail when you take off. Start looking for a likely small wave to promote a jump. When you see the right wave, luff to head straight at the ramp (**2**) shift your weight back and as you hit it lift with your front footstrap, flipping the board almost on the edge to get the wind underneath to promote the flight.

As the board takes off, pull down on the boom and bend your legs so that you lift the board with your feet (**3**). These must be firmly anchored in the straps by curled toes. With aggression, timing and strength you can use this technique to get the board into vertical take off – it's a bit like weightlifting, but it's over in a second.

The height and length of your flight can be prolonged by powering the rig, but it will make the board drift away downwind; you can reduce the effect by luffing the sail.

Coming back down from the VTO position, flatten the board (**4**) by pulling up sharply on the back footstrap and stretching out your front leg. This will also have the desirable effect of making the board bear off so that the nose is well down-wind of the tail, and there will be less likelihood of a spin-out on landing.

Landing relatively flat (**5**) will get the board going again quickly before the tail has a chance to sink. A very flat landing might break the board, so it should come down tail first and for preference on the windward rail. Use your feet and pull on the rig to control this. A nose dive must be avoided – just before touchdown luff the sail so that it doesn't pull you over.

Absorb the impact of landing by going into a squat, before straightening out and sailing on (**6**). If a spin-out seems unavoidable, transfer your weight on to the mastfoot and away from the back footstrap.

The technique for chop jumping is not as simple as it looks. The prime requisite is speed – if you're travelling at 25 knots it can be difficult to avoid getting airborne – plus control, strength and a 'go for it' attitude.

Wave Behaviour

At low tide the bottom shelves gently. The result is that the waves which break on the shoreline are insubstantial, and launching is therefore comparatively easy.

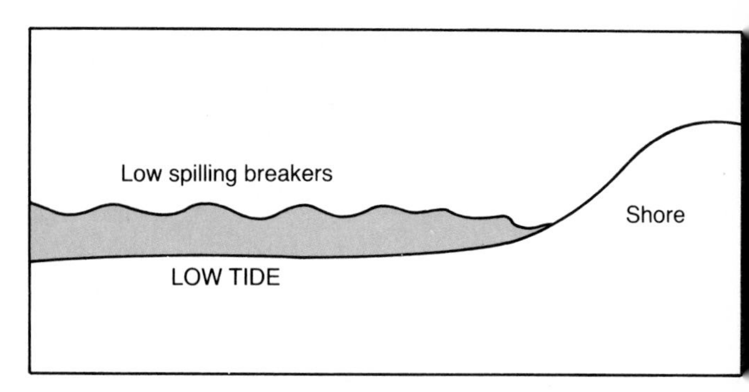

At high tide the picture changes and the waves heap up and 'dump' on the steeply shelving beach. Launching becomes difficult or even impossible. These conditions are typical of much of the UK's south coast.

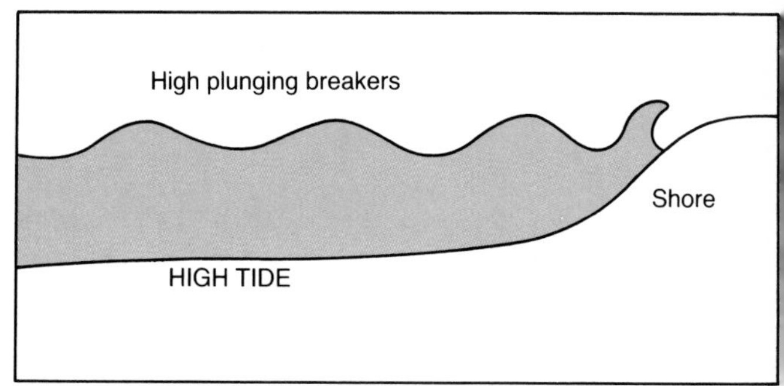

When the wind blows against the tide the waves are heaped up and the sea becomes violent and confused. Yachts can have a great deal of trouble in these conditions as they move so slowly against the oncoming tide – a windsurfer who falls off gets into even more trouble.

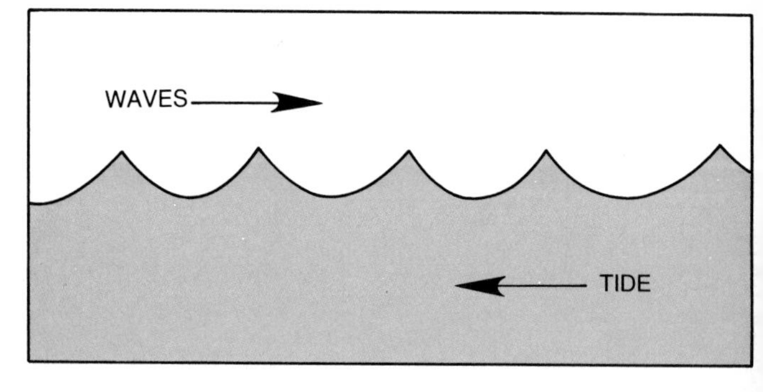

When the wind blows in the same direction as the tide, the sea is effectively flattened. Remember that the tide changes direction every six hours!

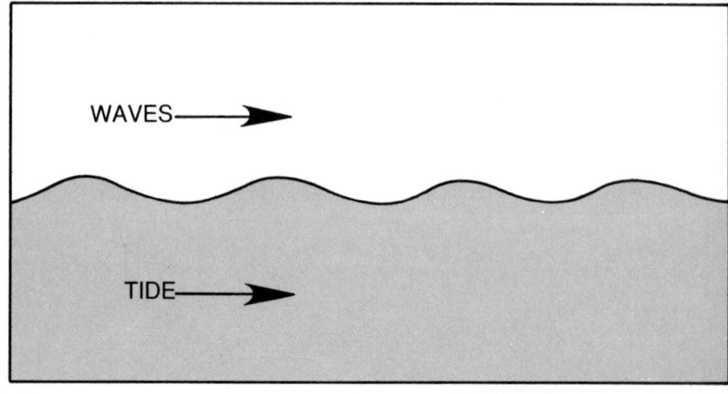

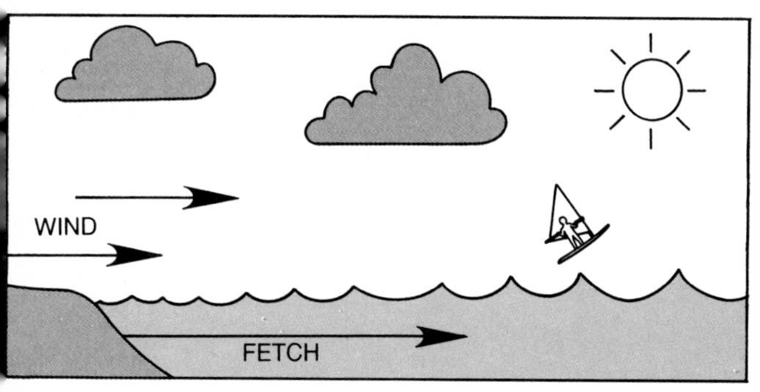

Beware the offshore wind. The longer the fetch out to sea, the stronger the wind and the bigger the waves. Hopping out may be easy but if you fall off you may find you can't handle the conditions.

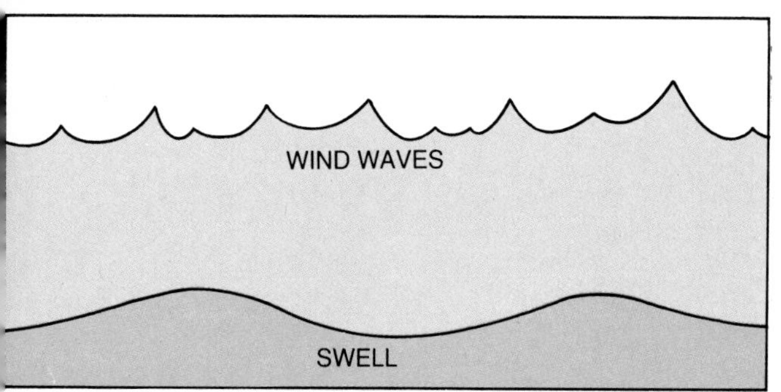

Wind generated waves are irregular and unpredictable when compared with an even swell. If there is a bump in the bottom, caused by a sand bar or reef, the waves will shoal and pile up even more violently.

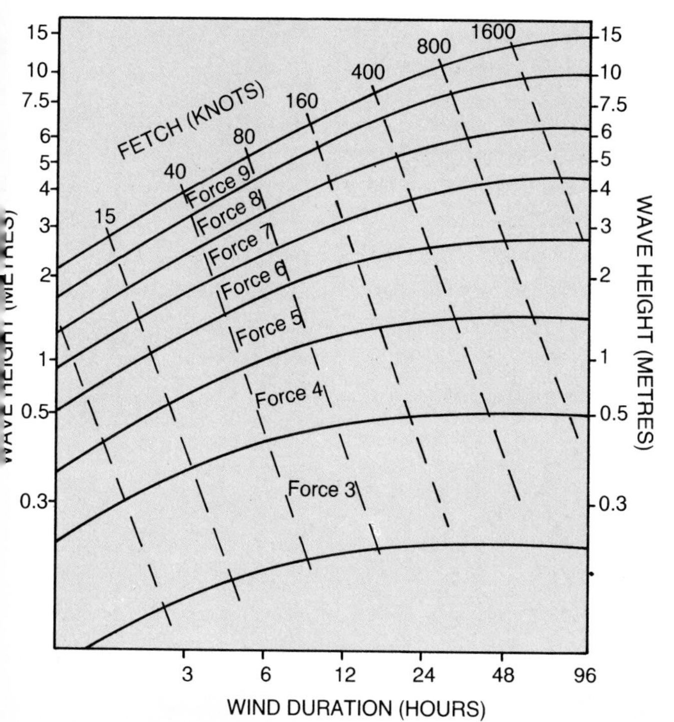

Simple Wave Forecasting

With a little research you can draw up and use a wave forecasting diagram. Try this example:

If the wind has been blowing Force 6 for 24 hours draw a vertical line from the 24 hour mark until you reach the Force 5 zone. Now draw two horizontal lines to the wave height scale, and read off the height of the wave – it will be one to 2.5 metres as long as the fetch is more than about 300 km. If the fetch is only 15 km, go down to the 15 km fetch dotted line, and the forecast waves will be only about one metre.

This method of wave forecasting is for the open sea, and ignores the changes waves undergo when they reach the coastline. The only way to allow for this is by using your own experience and local knowledge.

Understanding Waves

Waves are created in two ways before they hit the land: *ground swells* which are created by a storm and may travel thousands of kilometres across an ocean; and *wind swells* which are created when the wind blows for any length of time in one direction.

Hitting Land

Groundswell travels as a 'set', which is rather like a troop of soldiers. The set may contain as many as ten evenly spaced waves, with their speed governed by their length.

The waves in the set can only be dissipated when they hit something solid – usually land. They will break when the water shallows to a depth which is roughly $1\frac{1}{2}$ times the trough to crest height.

There are a variety of bottoms which cause waves to break:

Continental shelf. This is a relatively shallow sea bottom which extends some miles from the land before dropping suddenly into the ocean. It has the effect of decreasing the energy of the swell, and obvious examples are found off the Atlantic coasts of the UK and Europe.

When there is no shelf (such as Hawaii, which rises straight up from the ocean bed) the waves can hit the coast with force.

Reefs. A reef creates a sudden change from deep to shallow water. Upon hitting the reef, the swell will build up in height and break. If the change to shallow water is sudden, the base of the wave will slow more quickly than the top so that the top (or lip) throws itself out in front of the base and creates a 'tube'.

Beaches. If a sandy beach slopes gradually (usually at low tide) the waves will crumble slowly, from top to bottom. On a severely sloping beach (high tide), the waves will break violently and create 'dumpers' of white water.

Wind on Waves

Windsurfers are interested in waves when they hit land and wind effect is important:

Offshore. An offshore wind holds the waves up for longer than usual until they break along their length ('close out'). Great for surfing but dangerous for windsurfers.

Cross-offshore. Quite good for surfing and possible for windsurfing. Problems occur when the apparent wind created by the wave combines with the true wind. The effect may be an overpowering surge of wind on landing from a jump or making a top turn down the wave.

Sideshore. This can make chop across the faces of the waves with lips that crumble and go mushy. Overall, however, it's the best direction for wave-riding.

Cross-onshore. This is good for jumping. It's not so good for waveriding which is only possible with your back to the wave.

Onshore. Getting off the beach can be a nightmare. Once you're clear of the break the waves will tend to be all over the place and unpredictable. You can only ride the waves with your back to them ('backside').

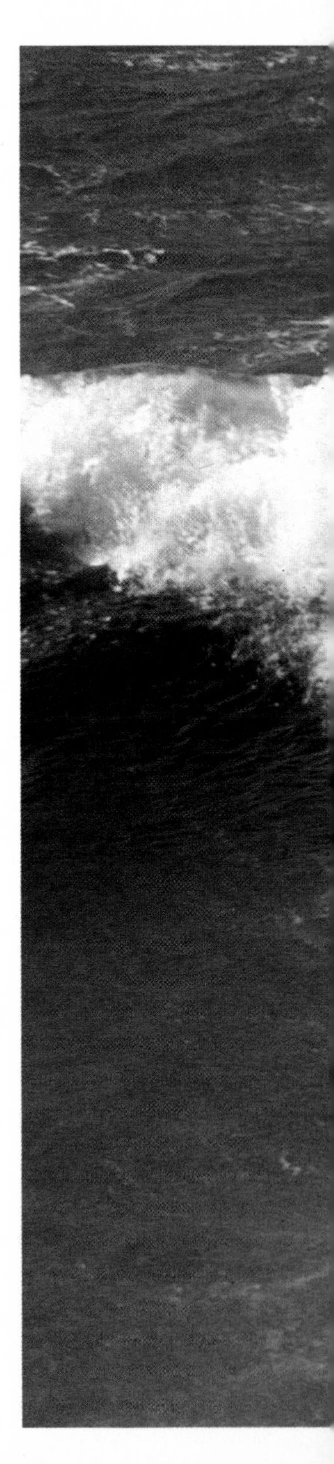

Hookipa probably has the world's most famous windsurfing waves.

Wave Manoeuvres

A wave will either peel to the right (the rider's right–'right break') or to the left (the rider's left–'left break').

The factors which govern where and how fast it will peel include its angle to the reef or sand bar. If the left-hand side of the wave is closer, it will break right; if the right hand side is closer it will break left; if the wave is parallel it will close out, peeling continuously along its length.

This diagram gives an idea of the variety of wavesailing available:

1. Wind.
2. Currents, which often create a short chop.
3. Offshore conditions. Ideal for surfing but no good for windsurfing.
4. Sideshore conditions – ideal for wavesailing.
5. Onshore and side onshore conditions.
6. *Backside bottom turn.* Board heads up into the wind and to the crest of the wave.
7. *Off the lip* or *top turn.* Board is projected down the face of the wave.
8. Reaching offwind at the bottom of the wave.
9. Side onshore jump. Board is luffed to meet wave squarely.
10. Riding *backside* into the wind.
11. Jump, with tail kicked upwind of the nose.
12. *Backside bottom turn.*
13. *Backside off the lip* for re-entry down the wave.
14. *Bottom turn* away from the wind.
15. *Top turn off the lip* for re-projection down the wave with the inside rail weighted, and the rig sheeted in and raked back.

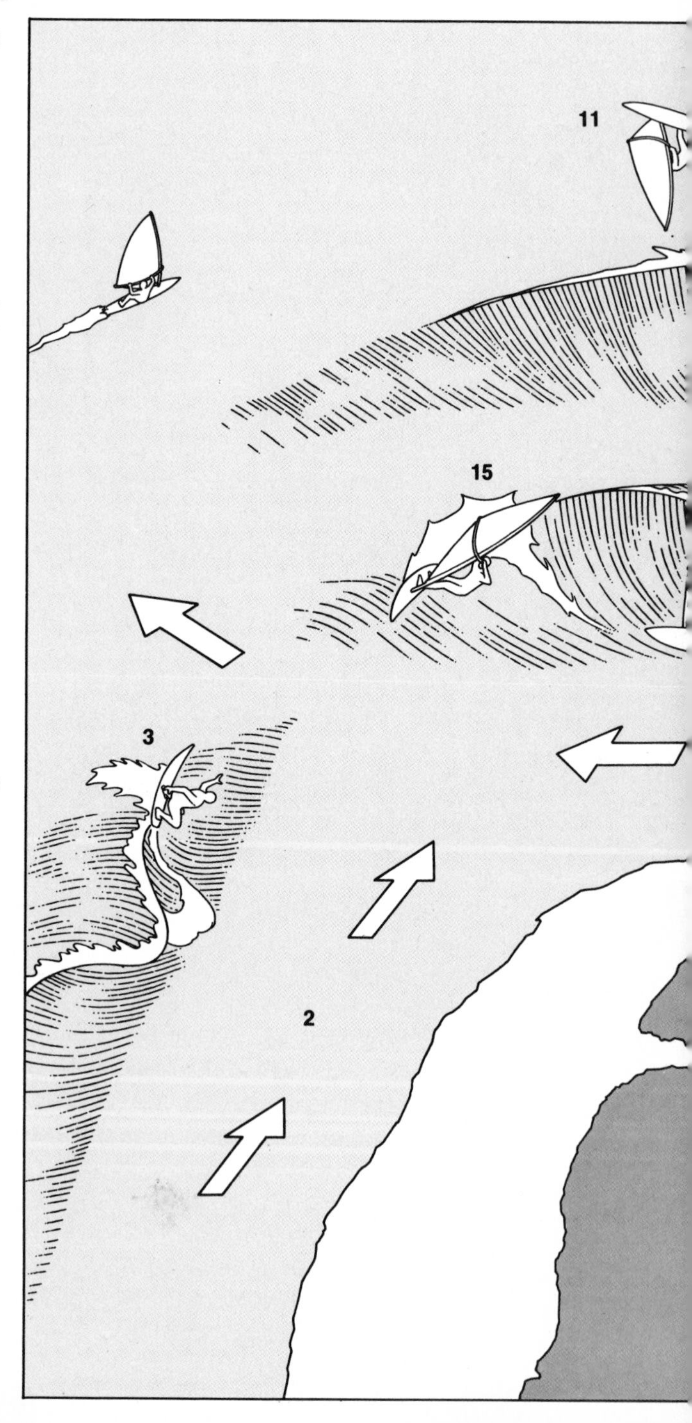

10
9
12
13
4
5
7
8
1
6

Top and Bottom Turns

Top and bottom turns are surfing manoeuvres which allow you to slalom along the length of the wave face. As you sail up the wave you top turn to sail back down, continuing the rollercoaster series of transitions until you have exhausted the face of the wave.

Top Turns

Sail the board up to the top of the wave, avoiding the part that's breaking. Just before you get there, put a lot of weight over the windward side tail of the board by leaning back with your body and the rig, sheeting in, and pushing down with the heel of your back foot. At the same time lift and pull with your front foot.

The board will make a tight turn to head back down the wave – as soon as it's on course, move your body weight forward and trim the rig to prevent it turning further.

Off the lip

This is the same turn but it's trickier as it's performed on the breaking lip of the wave.

Head up the wave as vertically as possible, and do your top turn when the breaking lip hits the underneath of the board. In big waves timing is critical to ensure the lip does not break over the leeward side of the sail.

Aerial off the lip

By going fast you can jump the board clear of the wave when the breaking lip hits the underneath. While in the air you must turn the board to head it back down the wave, landing on the face to continue sailing. Timing is absolutely crucial and this is a very difficult manoeuvre.

Backside Top Turns

Top turns are normally 'frontside' with your front facing the wave, as in the picture.

'Backside' is when the wind direction causes you to sail with your back to the wave face.

Top turning backside away from the lip is much the same as initiating a carve gybe – lift with your front foot, push down with the back one, and lean forward into the rig over the nose of the board.

A frontside (facing the wave) top turn will take the sailor back down the face of the wave. He depresses the inner rail, sheets in and rakes back the rig. The wind is sideshore but the apparent wind created by his speed and the wave puts him on a close reach.

Bottom Turns

The bottom turn is performed at high speed at the base of the wave. Due to the speed there may be problems with spin-out and lack of control (see the section about Asymmetrics on pages 22–23). The timing and positioning of the turn will to a large extent determine where you have to make a top turn, which might be the wrong or right part of the wave. Bottom turns can be made frontside (facing the wave) or backside (back to the wave):

Frontside, the turn is begun in the same way as a carve gybe with the board speed, wave speed, and true wind speed combining to put the board on to a broad reach even though it's travelling downwind. Having made the turn, you can either shoot off diagonally downwind and up across the face, or continue the turn until you are headed straight back up the wave for an off the lip top turn.

Backside bottom turns are made when the wind is more onshore than sideshore, and you can't get enough power sailing frontside. When you reach the bottom of the wave you pull your weight back over the tail to stall the board and carve it back up the face. It's considerably slower and less control critical than the frontside bottom turn (which is shown in the illustration below) with the sailor about to head back up the wave face.

Competition

Regatta Gear

The equipment needed for a funboard regatta becomes complex when there are three disciplines and the weather is an unknown quantity.

At World Cup level the equipment becomes super complex, as Hi Fly racer Bjorn Schrader demonstrates with this line-up of the gear needed for one World Cup regatta in Hawaii.

Sails

Anything up to 8 sq m for course racing in the minimum 15 knot wind speed. Anything down to 3 sq m with super short booms for waveriding.

Masts and Booms

Masts get broken, and the top racer carries a lot of them. With high aspect sails they need to range from super short for tiny waveriding sails, up to super long (5.25 m plus) for the big course racing sails. Even then they may not be long enough and a variety of adjustable extensions are often necessary.

Booms get broken as well and the non-adjustable type have the best stiffness-to-weight ratio for the serious racer.

Boards

Two race boards flank two slalom boards with a wave-riding board in the middle. All are custom made by Hi Fly designer Helmut Kirner, using epoxy/polystyrene construction for the long boards and epoxy/polyurethane for short boards.

The design of boards changes constantly and a wave sailing specialist will have many to choose from.

Adventure-Wear
G 9
HOOD
HOOD
Audi
quattro
HOOD

Funboard Regattas

The Races

Wind and weather permitting, the three major disciplines in a funboard regatta are Course Racing, Slalom and Wave Riding. They count for 40%, 40% and 20% respectively towards the overall results.

This is the system used by the WSMA for the prestigious World Cup circuit which first started in 1983. The principles of the system remain the same for lesser events as long as the right wind and water conditions exist.

Course Racing

Each discipline needs different equipment and requires different skills. Course racing is most similar to the conventional style of triangle racing. The main difference between the two is the emphasis on reaching and gybing in course racing while beating to windward is minimized.

Racing Boards

The boards used for course racing have evolved from Hawaii's Pan Am Cup. They need to give maximum performance on the reaches and manoeuvrability enough to gybe through the slalom part of the course. They must also have full length daggerboards

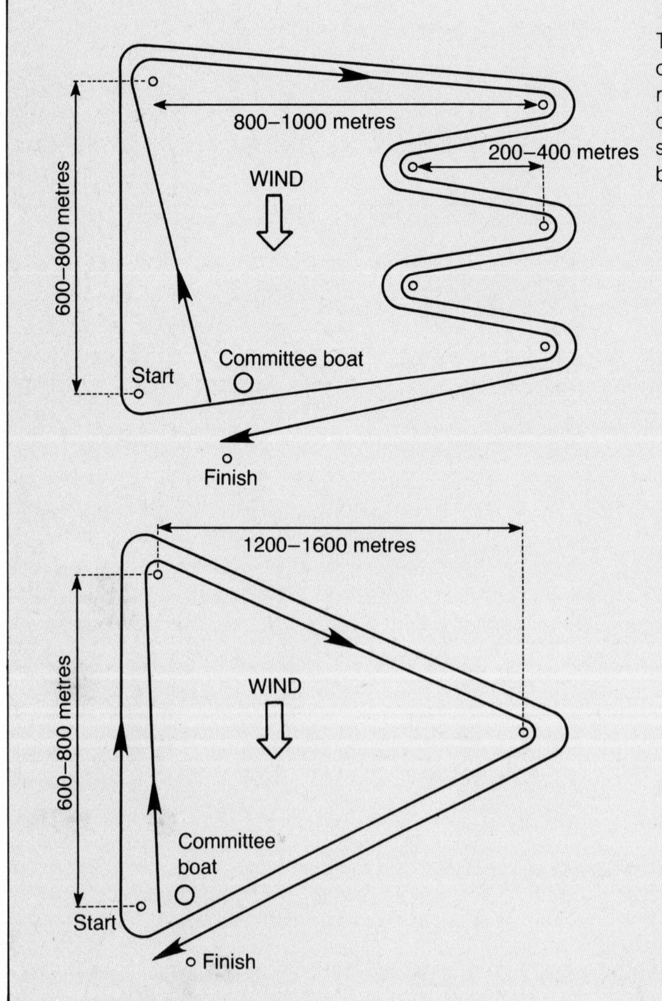

The standard course race (left) is often called the 'Giant Slalom'. In rough conditions it may be too difficult to lay all the marks and a simpler course (below left) must be used.

and mast tracks to get them up the short windward legs.

The boards vary in length from 3.6 m to 3.7 m and carry rigs of up to 7 sq m.

Top sailors on the World Cup circuit invariably use prototypes. Some of these boards are turned into popular production boards. Some examples of these are the Mistral Malibu, Fanatic Racy Cup and Tiga Fun Cup.

The Course

The course follows the same line as a conventional Olympic Triangle starting with a short beat or fetch to the first mark. Then the competitors must bear away or tack round the mark, kick up the daggerboard and pull back the mast track for the long reach across the top of the course.

The slalom section then starts with a gybe, followed by four more gybes in quick succession, before a reach across the bottom of the course. Then comes another lap or the finish depending on conditions.

The standard Giant Slalom course may be impossible to set, in which case the race committee design their own course to suit wind and waves.

The Rules

The main rule is a minimum wind speed of 15 knots (WSMA). Otherwise the object is to get round the course as fast as possible. Although rules are based on the IYRU, marks can be touched, pumping is allowed and protests are discouraged.

Ken Winner racing for Bic in the Course Racing of the World Cup circuit at San Francisco. Ken was second to Robby Naish in the overall placings for the first World Cup in 1983.

Slalom

Slalom is probably the favourite discipline in a funboard regatta. It's simple and it's very fast and, as long as there's enough wind, it's easy to lay an appropriate course for racing.

Figure-of-Eight Course

Sometimes the slalom is referred to as 'Ins-and-Outs'. This term has been handed down from the Pan Am Cup where racing was held in and out through the surf on a course similar to the figure-of-eight in the diagram below.

Even when conditions are less than perfect, some kind of slalom event, with high speed reaching and gybing, can always be held. The course can be varied to suit local conditions.

The best course, however, is a figure-of-eight with surf between the two marks.

The Boards

Boards used for slalom are invariably short. Sometimes, however, in certain conditions sailors will opt for marginals of around 2.9 m with enough buoyancy to keep them planing through the lulls.

Plan Shape

Favourite plan shape tends towards the long, slim gun. Double concave underwater shape is preferred for acceleration. Emphasis has also to be given to good gybing performance with sharp railed, low volume tails.

Slalom Rigs

Rigs need to be powerful for instant acceleration out of the gybes. But when all is said and done the main requirements are skill and aggression.

The Course

With short boards, slalom racing is ideally started and finished Le Mans style on the beach. The sailors line up at the water's edge, the gun goes off and they rush into the water to start their boards. At the finish they sail in, jump off and run up the beach.

Below: An alternative WSMA slalom course gives the option of (1) starting on the water and finishing on the beach, (2) starting on the beach and finishing on the water or (3) starting and finishing on water. The length of the course may vary, with as many as eight gybe marks in succession. This course is obviously much more difficult to lay than the simple, standard course.

Right: The standard slalom course is the simplest and best. The tactical problem is that competitors have to sail close reaches. As soon as they round the top or bottom mark they have to aim well to windward if they are to get round the next mark. If they fall off and get blown downwind they are out of the race as the winner speeds home, a slalom race is invariably over in a matter of minutes.

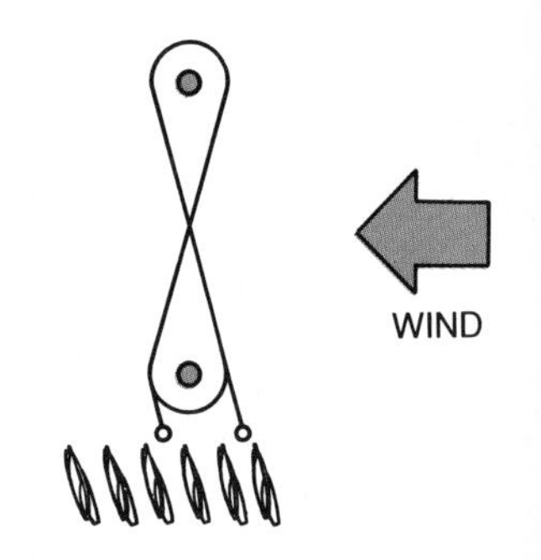

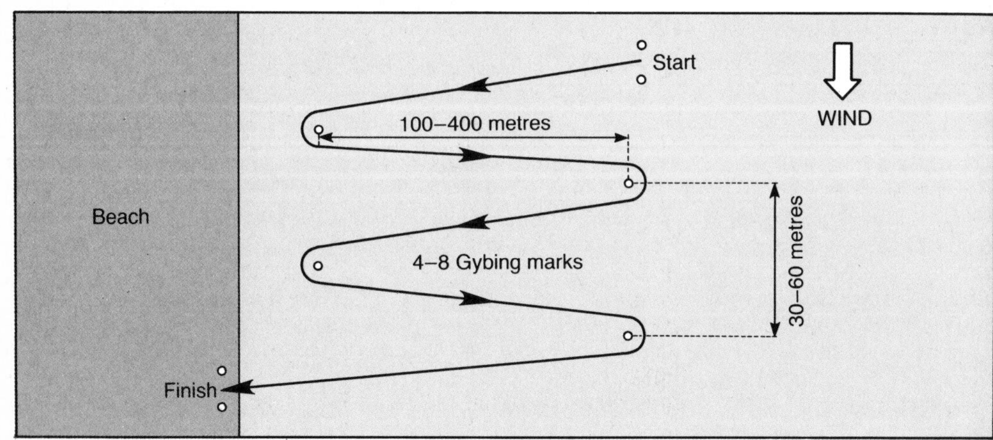

Waterstarts
With a strong onshore wind it may be impossible to start in this style and so the start has to be on water. This causes several problems for the competitors who are sailing sinkers. Waterstarting and hitting the line at full speed – all done just at the right second – require excellent judgement and a lot of practice.

There are generally a maximum of eight competitors in a slalom race. A series is held over a day or more on a knock-out basis. The front runners go on to the next rounds and so on until the final is reached.

'Man-on-Man'
Where there are a limited number of competitors the slalom may be run 'man-on-man', that is with just two sailors in each heat.

Rules
The wind speed should be a minimum of 18 knots over the course area (WMSA) for the men and a minimum of 15 knots for the women.

Competitors enter an elimination ladder with four out of eight starters advancing to the next heat. Alternatively, they can race 'man-on-man' with the winner of each heat progressing to the next round.

The losers may have their own ladder and the winner of the 'losers' race can meet the winner of the 'winners' in a final race.

Why are they called 'Ins-and-Outs'? On the way out through the surf, racing boards may get airborne and hop in and out of the water from wave top to wave top. On the way back, they shoot down each wave face at helter-skelter speed before gybing to make the next reach out again.

Course Rules
Rules of the course are simple:
1. All marks must be rounded but no penalty for touching them.
2. A competitor going out against the waves has right of way over one coming in with the waves.
3. A competitor clear astern keeps away from one clear ahead. He also keeps clear while overtaking.

Wave Riding

Wave riding requires good waves, a minimum 12 knot wind (WSMA), and two competitors who put on their own freestyle display on the waves.

At the end of each heat (either five, eight or 12 minutes) the judges choose the winner who then goes on to the next winners heat.

The loser goes on to the next losers heat, and at the end the winner of the 'winners' takes on the best of the 'losers' to find the overall victor.

The Boards

Short wavesailing boards are generally used, but size is decided by the wind conditions. For example, a 2.5 m sinker is ultra-manoeuvrable in 30 knots but it will sink in the troughs. On the other hand, a sailor on a more floaty marginal style board, can keep going in troughs and, as he reaches higher speeds, will be able to perform good jumps.

Top sailors are liable to turn up at a World Cup event with two or three different boards so that they can pick the best one for the prevailing conditions on the day.

The Course

The course is determined by the field of vision of the judges (see diagram below). A sailor may be doing brilliant jumps and gybes, but it's no good if he can't be seen.

Points

Normally there are three or five judges who decide the winner. Each judge awards each competitor up to ten points for a wave ride, ten points for a jump and five points for a transition. Then the scores are totalled.

Rules

Some rules are necessary to decide who has right of way:

1. The competitor coming in with the wave keeps clear of the competitor going out.

2. The first competitor to get on a wave has 'possession'.

3. Two competitors may sail the same wave but the one with possession has right of way.

4. When not on a wave, a competitor in transition (gybing) keeps clear of the other.

5. If two competitors are both in transition, the one on the other's port side keeps clear.

6. A competitor clear astern must keep out of the way.

7. An overtaking competitor must keep clear.

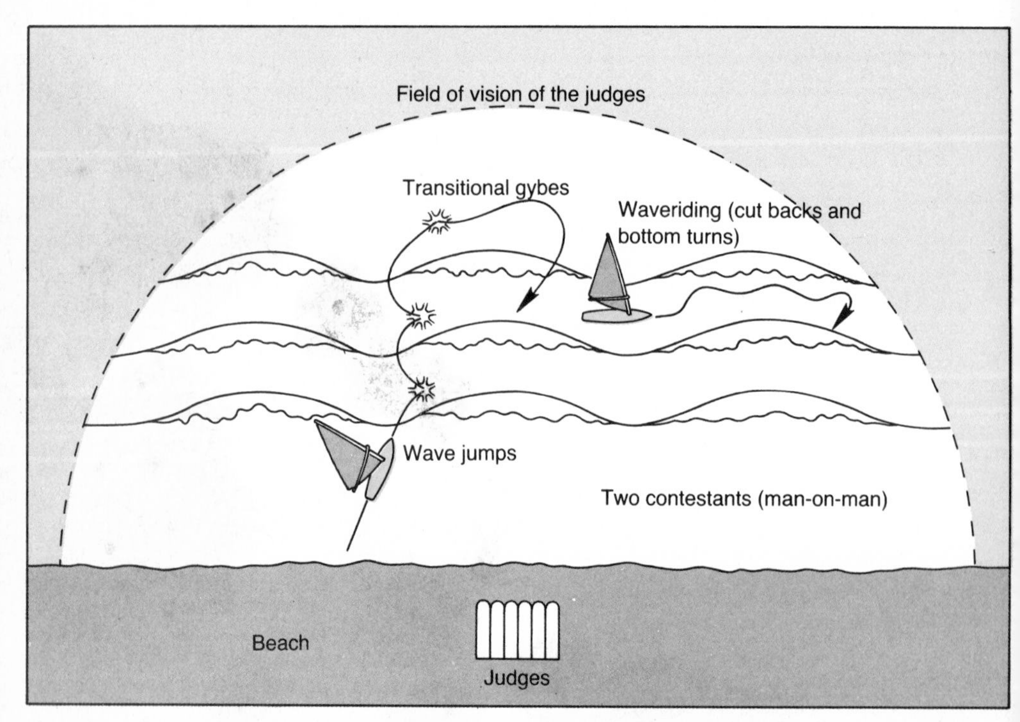

Speed Trials

The contest to become the fastest windsurfer in the world is growing in popularity. The time may not be far off when a board becomes the fastest sailing craft in the world. At present the record stands at 36 knots which the British proa, *Crossbow II*, set in Portland Harbour in 1979.

Weymouth Speed Trials

The concept of having a 500 metre course to measure the speed of sailing craft originated at the Weymouth Speed Trials.

These are held in Portland Harbour, near Weymouth on the south coast of England. To date the trials have claimed the majority of world records – and windsurfers are gradually encroaching upon the speed records of more conventional craft.

World Record Holders

The windsurfing world speed record holders are as follows:

1977

Derk Thijs (Netherlands) ran at 17.1 knots in Portland. He used a standard (Olympic) Windglider with the daggerboard slot sealed and foam removed to make it lighter.

1979

Clive Colenso (UK) sailed his own design, Olympic Gold, to 19.2 knots at Portland.

1980

Jaap van der Rest (Netherlands) stayed on with an observer after the first (and only) Maalaea Speed Trials on the island of Maui (Hawaii). He eventually recorded 24.45 knots on a board specially designed by Gary Seaman.

1981

Jürgen Hönscheid (W. Germany) took a surfboard gun, attached rig and footstraps and pushed the record up to 24.75 knots at Portland. It was the first appearance of a sinker in this type of event but since then they have dominated all speed events.

A few months later Jaap van der Rest won back the record (25.2 knots) sailing his own design sinker at the Dutch Speed Trials at Veere.

1982

Philip Pudenz (W. Germany) had a short-lived reign when he pushed the record to just over 26 knots at Brest Speed Week, held in Brest Harbour in north-west France. Within a couple of weeks Pascal Maka (France) had set a new record of 27.82 knots in Portland.

1983

Fred Haywood (USA) came to Portland with a special team from Hawaii and set a new record of 30.82 knots.

Venues and Rules

So long as the board is wind propelled there are no restrictions placed on equipment used to attempt the World Speed Record, although there are classes that are largely determined by sail area.

The conditions most favourable for record breaking are flat water, a minimum of 30 knots wind speed and a very broad reach.

The 500 metre course is set with time-keepers or timing devices at each end and a RYA observer to ratify the new record. This can only be claimed if it exceeds the previous by 2%.

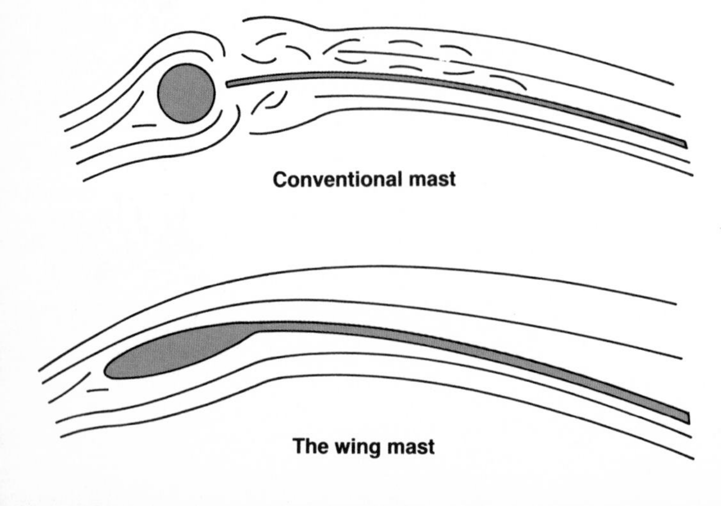

Fred Haywood was the first sailor to make successful use of a wing mast. This design creates less turbulence than the conventional round mast.

The 'Wing' was made by American engineer Dimitri Milovich. It was used with sails made by Barry Spanier of Maui Sails and sponsored by Neil Pryde.

Although the wing works well on one track speed sailing, it demands such precise tuning and trimming that it is not likely to be much use for more general forms of windsurfing in the near future.

Above: Fred Haywood is a big, powerful sailor who used a very small board to break the record – it was shaped for his company (Sailboards Maui) by Jimmy Lewis. Note the unusually wide wishbone which enables Fred to lean right back with the rig upright for maximum power. He gets further leverage on the rig with a trapeze wire which is led from a point at two-thirds mast height down to his harness.

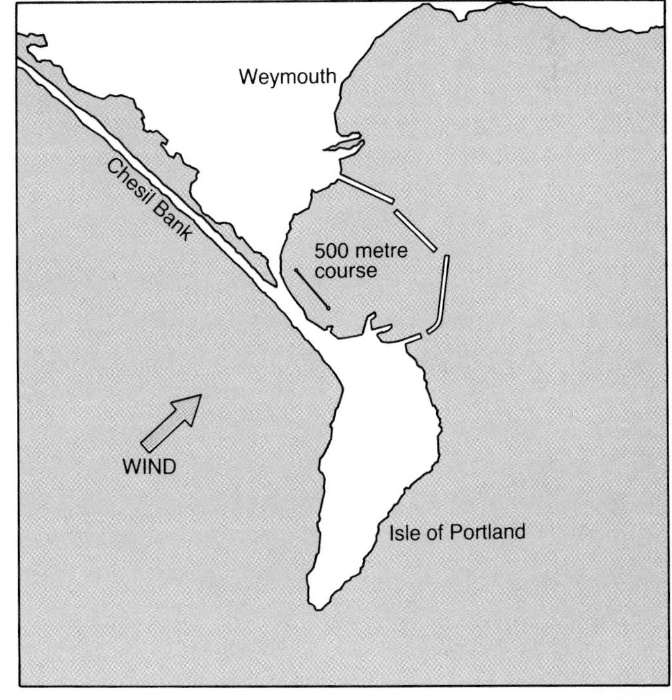

Right: Portland Harbour has consistently provided the world's best speed trial conditions. The autumn equinoctial gales blow from the west and have an uninterrupted path up the English Channel until they hit the Chesil Bank. This huge bank of shingle has the effect of accelerating the wind so that it hits the calm inshore water of Portland Harbour with maximum ferocity.

Custom Boards

Custom Airbrush

Custom boards become an art form when the skill of the air-brush designer can be seen through the clear glassfibre skin.

Designs such as these don't do anything to affect the board's performance – they are purely for the satisfaction of the customer and, predictably, add considerably to the cost.

Custom board manufacture evolved from the surfboard business and is concentrated on the popular surfing areas in Australia, Hawaii and the West Country of England.

These three boards show the sophistication of British airbrush technique. The top board is one of a pair of asymmetrics by Chapter. In the middle is a Brainwaves board specially designed for mushy waves and, at the bottom, a Circle One in the style of Alan Jones.

Custom Construction

Custom construction is the back-bone of windsurfing. It's the way in which virtually all the prototypes are made, tried and tested. Also, when a major manufacturer decides on the final shape of a new model, a custom board is used as the first stage of making the moulds.

Shaping

Custom boards are always built in much the same way although there are sometimes slight variations.

The shaper starts with a foam 'blank' which is roughly the shape and size of the board to be made. It's usually polyurethane foam (Clark of the USA is one of the best known brands). Sometimes polystyrene foam is used. It is lighter and cheaper but much more difficult to work with and it's not likely to make much difference to the all-up weight of a low volume short board.

The foam blank is usually made up with one or two plywood stringers to give it (and the finished board) rigidity down the centreline.

A shaper's tools are a saw, an electric planer and sandpaper blocks, ranging from rough to the finest grades. The shaping is generally done by eye alone, using the shaper's skill and experience. A couple of fluorescent lights can be mounted on either side of the board to throw shadow on any unevenness but, unless the work is being done to specific designs, the shaper is unlikely to use templates.

The shaper begins by taking the hard skin off the bottom of the foam with the electric planer. He then cuts out the plan shape of the board with the saw, works on the bottom shape and finally shapes the deck and rails.

Depending on the complexity of the shape, a skilled shaper can get from blank to finished shape in around 40 minutes – fancy variations such as channels and wingers will take a lot longer.

Airbrushing

Most custom boards are laminated with a hard glassfibre cloth and polyester resin skin which is transparent.

This means you can see through to the foam which is airbrushed to give the board its design and colours.

Airbrushing is done with cellulose car paint. It may take anything from ten minutes to several days depending on the complexity of the design. If the design is a geometric one it is usual to mask off areas and spray the exposed parts of the board until the required effect is built up. If the design is more figurative (see the boards on the previous pages), a highly qualified artist will be employed.

Laminating

The airbrush paint dries almost immediately and the next stage is to laminate the board with glassfibre cloth and polyester resin. These form the hard, outer coat.

The laminator has to be a quick and competent worker as the laminate can harden within 15 minutes. First he laminates the bottom of the board with two layers which are cut to shape around the rails. Then the resin is poured on and is spread over the glassfibre with a squeegee. It is important to use as little resin as possible to impregnate the glassfibre so that the weight is kept down. It is equally important to avoid air bubbles.

After about two hours the bottom will be sufficiently hard. The board is turned over and trimmed round the rails. Then three layers are laminated on to the deck, with an overlap on the rails that has to be resined on to the bottom layer.

Extra layers of glass cloth are invariably added as reinforcement under the footstraps and the mast track area. Some boards are laminated with 'exotic' cloths such as Kevlar or carbon fibre but the general opinion is that boards can be made light and strong enough without recourse to materials that shoot up the price.

Fittings

The next stage is to put in the fin boxes and the mast track. The slots are routed out and the pre-moulded polycarbonate boxes are wrapped in a layer of glass and resined into position.

Finishing

This is the most labour-intensive part of the whole operation. After the glassfibre laminate has fully cured it is power sanded. A shiny finish coat of resin mixed with wax is applied and this is polished with increasingly fine grades of wet and dry sandpaper. Finally it is buffed with car polish on a lambswool pad.

The footstraps are then resined or bolted in place on the deck.

Shaping: The shaper turns the foam blank into a perfectly symmetrical board shape using power tools, his experience and his 'eye'.

Airbrushing: The shaped blank is painted with an airbrush spray. The finished design will be seen clearly through the glass laminate.

Laminating: Glassfibre cloth is laminated with the polyester resin which reacts to turn it into the hard glass outer skin.

Finishing: Having put in the fin boxes and mast track, the final gleaming finish is achieved by hours of careful polishing.

The Best Funboard Places

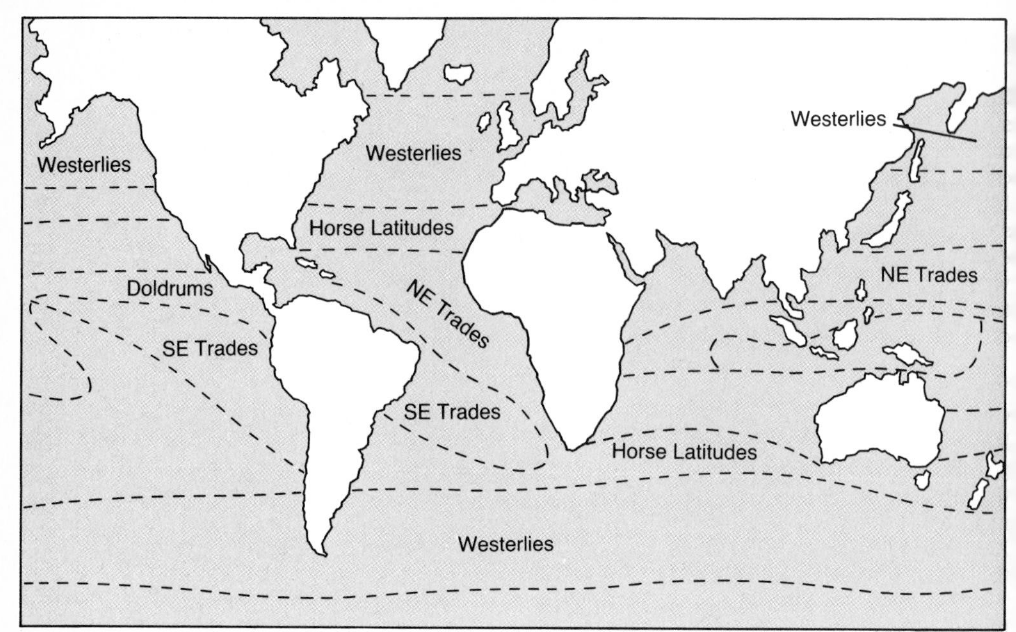

Above: The major wind systems of the world are dominated by the Trade Winds which are reliable and thus the favourites of windsurfers. They blow from the Horse Latitudes to the Doldrums, north-easterly in the Northern Hemisphere and south-easterly in the Southern Hemisphere. The winds move with the sun, south or north according to season. The Trade Winds blow over both the Caribbean and Hawaii.

Below: The strong Mediterranean winds are at their most potent on hot summer afternoons. In the east the Meltemi can be guaranteed to blow Force 4 or more day after day around the Greek islands. In the west the Straits of Gibraltar accelerate the winds from both east and west. These have helped establish Tarifa, on the southernmost tip of Spain, as a premier windsurfing location with year round sideshore conditions.

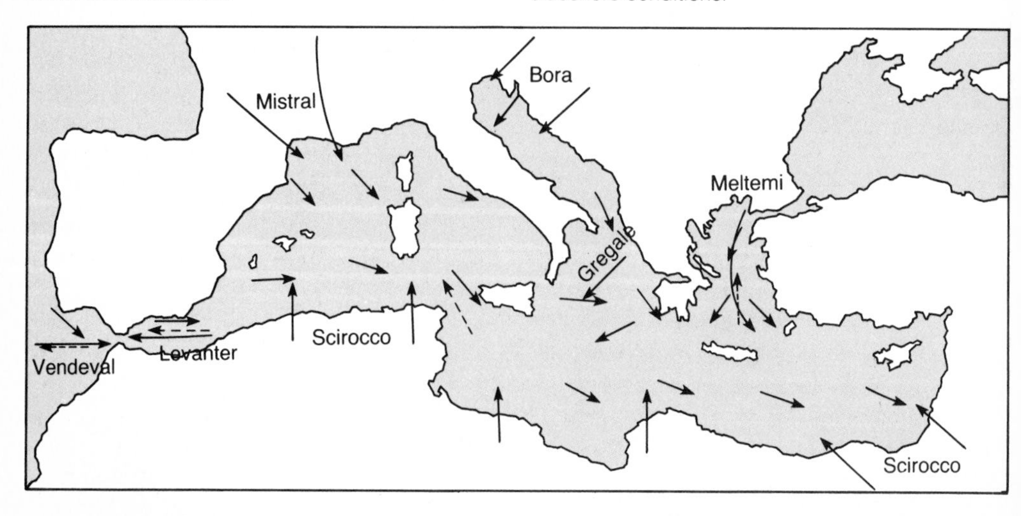

Hawaii

The Hawaiian islands have become the mecca of windsurfing because, when conditions are good, they are very good. Warm 20 knot winds blow sideshore along with stunning waves to create the exhibition areas for the best wave sailors – if you want to test your skills against the big guys, Hawaii is the place to go.

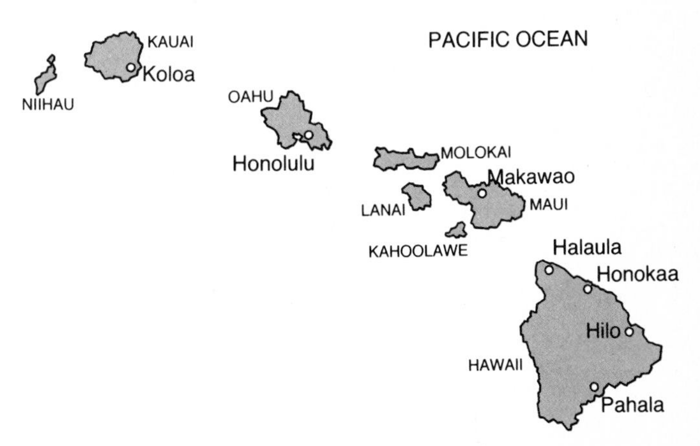

Niihau is known as The Private Isle and is privately owned. Kauai is known as The Garden Isle and is very lush. Oahu is known as The Gathering Place. It has 80% of the population and the major airport. Molokai is known as The Friendly Isle, and is a good long distance sail from Maui. Lanai is known as The Pineapple Island – and that's what it is. Kahoolawe is known as The Deadly Island, and is strictly military. Maui is known as The Valley Island, and is a short plane ride from Oahu. It's much quieter than Oahu and boasts the Haleakala volcano. Hawaii is known as The Big Island and has famous volcanoes.

Which Island?

Oahu is the most heavily populated island with about 800,000 people, most of whom live in the city of Honolulu. The three most popular places to sail are Kailua Bay, Diamond Head and the North Shore.

Kailua Bay used to be the home of the Pan Am World Cup. It is a protected bay with a beautiful sandy beach where the water can be calm or rough depending on the wind. Inside the bay you'll find small swells and clear water. A little further out beyond Flat Island you may be challenged by bigger swells which are sometimes big enough for jumping.

Whilst there you will see the most famous windsurfers' shops anywhere – *Naish Hawaii* and *Windsurfing Hawaii*, just across the street from one another.

Diamond Head is the place to go if you are used to short boards and are proficient at waterstarting. Although it is very shallow because of the coral heads, the reef creates ideal waves. A disadvantage is the long walk down the hill to the beach. Also be warned that it's never safe to leave valuables unattended while you're sailing. Best conditions occur in summer, when there are steady Trade winds and a good swell from the south.

The North Shore is famous for the Pipeline and Sunset waves that are legendary in the world of surfing. The best section of the break for windsurfing is Backyards, with the best sailing in summer. However, the biggest waves occur in late autumn and early winter.

Maui is the place for those who prefer to get away from it all. Due to the mountain formations here the winds are reckoned to be better than Oahu, with the most reliable conditions found from July to November. The three favourite places are Kanaha, Spreckleville and Hookipa.

Kanaha Beach Park has a soft white sandy beach and a large area of flat water which is ideal for beginners and less experienced sailors. You can warm up on the sheltered side of the reef and then head further out to the breaking waves when you feel more confident. They're small waves by Hawaiian standards but big in comparison to elsewhere.

Sprecklesville has bigger waves and is a good place for experienced short board sailors to practise waveriding. However, the main place is Hookipa which is ofen considered to be the ultimate windsurfing stomping ground.

What to take

The Hawaiian sun is intense, so sunburn can be a problem. You don't need much in the way of clothes but a short wetsuit or vest can be useful. It's also worth bearing in mind that coral cut infections on your feet could ruin your trip.

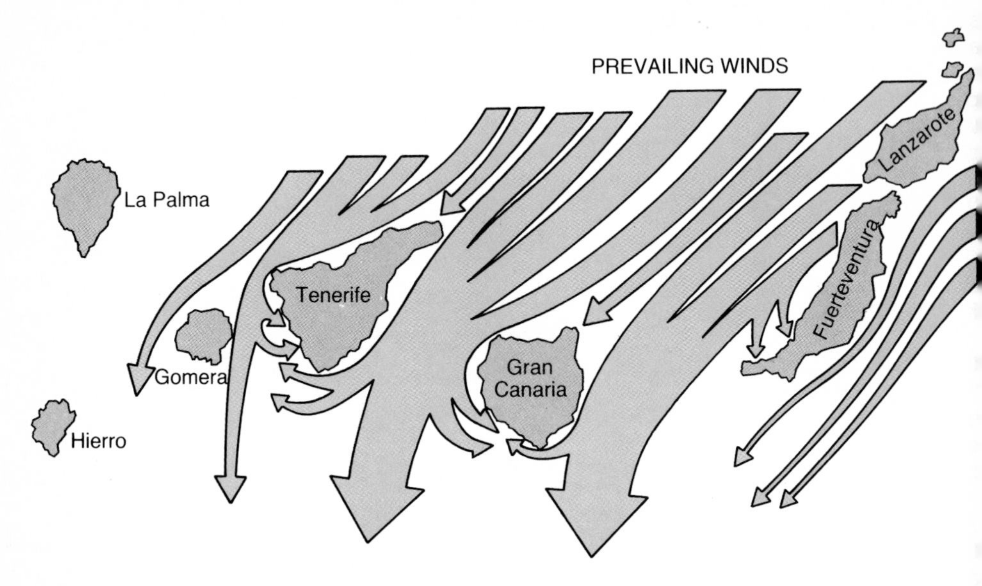

The Canaries

The Spanish Canary Islands are situated just off the west African coast. This region is the nearest to mainland Europe which has the right mix of sun and wind for most of the year.

The sun is guaranteed and the North East Trade Winds funnel between the island, accelerating along the coasts, to give some exciting windsurfing conditions. The best time for wind is definitely in the summer. In winter you probably still have a 50:50 chance of getting what you want.

At present the best known windsurfing islands are Lanzarote, Fuerteventura and Gran Canaria. Tenerife is also beginning to become a popular venue.

Lanzarote and Fuerteventura have volcanic origins and are largely composed of sand and rock with sparse vegetation. Fuerteventura has the better sideshore conditions and most of the windsurfing action is centred round the small town of Corralejo in the north-east of the island, where there are magnificent waves offshore.

Gran Canaria is altogether more of a tourist's island but has good winds where the wind sweeps round its southern tip. The coastline is uninspiring but there is a large Club Mistral at the holiday village of Bahia Feliz. This is an excellent place for a cheap windsurfing holiday. It is also within easy reach of the mountainous centre of the island which boasts some stunning scenery.

Italy

The 65 km long Lake Garda in northern Italy is the most popular windsurfing spot in central Europe.

Sited half-way between Milan and Venice, it's within easy reach of Austria and Germany. On a sunny weekend in summer you can expect to see around 4000 boards on the water.

Apart from being in a pleasant, easily accessible area, much of its popularity stems from its reliable winds. Mountains surround the lake on three sides and they provide regular thermal breezes with a basic pattern: The light moderate Vento blows from the north in the morning. In the middle of the day there is a period of calm. In the afternoon the strong Ora blows Force 6–7 from the south.

All over the lake area there are a variety of thermal breezes, but the Ora is the most powerful on the northern part of the lake where the windsurfing 'capitals' are the towns of Torbole and Riva, and the villages of Limone and Malcesine.

The season lasts from spring to November. Hotels and campsites abound on the lake shores and all offer board storage facilities.

There are also well over twenty windsurfing schools in the region and stars such as Heinz Stickl (ex World and European Champion) and Michiel Bouwmeester offer everything from basics to advanced tuition.

Lake Garda is also well

served by windsurfing shops and custom board manufacturers. Most of the big European board makers use the lake as a testing ground. It is a good place to keep an eye on trends in the market. During the summer it's usual to find the trendsetters based nearby – (Hansi Fichtner/F2, Charly and Rolf Messmer/Mistral, Helmut Kirner/Hi Fly, etc).

United Kingdom

The hottest area for funboard sailing in the UK is undoubtedly the West Country. The coasts of Devon and Cornwall stretch straight out into the Atlantic and receive the full force of the westerly winds and waves that have built up over hundreds of kilometres of open sea.

These factors made the coastline a premier European surfing location before windsurfing came on the scene. So there were already a score of surfboard shapers and wetsuit manufacturers who were able to adapt their skills easily to the new sport.

As a result, the West Country is the centre of British funboard manufacture, with a variety of famous names producing custom and moulded boards. In Cornwall, Redruth plays host to Limited Edition while Vitamin Sea and Ocean Magic are a little further up the coast in Newquay. In Devon, Braunton has been transformed into a windsurfing town, with Chapter, Tiki, Surfline, New Waves and Hy Jumpers amongst the makers in and around the area.

What of the sailing? Cornwall has the advantage in that you can drive from coast to coast in little more than half-an-hour. It is always possible to move to the best beaches for the prevailing wind.

North Devon has the best beaches of all. The magnificent stretches of sand at Saunton and Woolacombe are ideally placed for sideshore sailing in south westerly winds.

Australia

Western Australia is recognized for its windsurfing excellence. The vast area of dry desert sucks in a south-westerly sea breeze from the Indian Ocean which provides port tack jumping all along the north–south coastline.

However, Western Australia has a huge coastline, about 2000 km from north to south and 1600 km from West to East. The best starting point from the point of view of windsurfers is probably Perth, where there is a good windsurfing population. You should make expeditions from there to Lanceton and Geraldton (both about 500 km distant) where there are excellent reef breaks.

The best time to visit Australia is from November to March. After that you need to move northwards to stay with the high pressure areas. In the Perth region and most of the south the high pressure is replaced by a low pressure belt of cloud and rain.

Caribbean

A relatively narrow belt in the southern Caribbean gets good, reliable Trade Winds which blow at a steady 12 knots plus.

Among the islands best served by the Trades are the Virgin Islands (the 'Hang In and Hook On' is an excellent annual ten day race round the islands), and the Leeward and Windward Islands. Guadeloupe (France) and Barbados (UK) have both held major world championships.

South Africa

Inland South Africa has plenty of potential venues for windsurfing but, unfortunately, many of the large, dammed lakes are less than half full in times of severe drought and are invariably subject to restrictions. The favourite inland place for sailing is the Vaal Dam, just south-east of Johannesburg, although it has only light winds in the summer (September to February).

The best conditions are inevitably on the coast where the sailing can be excellent in both summer and winter seasons. All the east coast is good, and main windsurfing centres include Durban and Capetown.

Launch places worth particular mention are the Point Yacht Club at Durban; Hobie Beach and Jeffrey's Bay (mainly surfing) at Port Elizabeth; and Blonberg Strand at Capetown, where the Gunston Surfsailing International attracts some of the best foreign sailors every Christmas.

South African windsurfing weather is generally extremely hot in summer but surprisingly chilly in winter.

Canada

The big lakes of Canada have enough wind-blown chop to give good funboarding conditions.

Jackson's Point on Lake Simco is rated as a 'mini Hawaii', while the enormous Lake Eyrie is also popular.

Canadians also compete in one of windsurfing's great events, the Columbia Gorge Pro-Am Speed Slalom, held just across the border in the USA. The Gorge has consistent 20–35 knot winds.

Self-Preservation

Self-Rescue

It's unfortunate that self-rescue is sometimes necessary. It is usually occasioned by equipment failure or by the sailor being caught by sudden weather changes.

Wind Too Strong

If the wind becomes too strong and you have equipment failure or just can't handle it, then you are likely to have problems.

Rolling up the rig and paddling home against a 25 knot wind may prove impossible, and you will wish that:

You had told someone to keep an eye on you.

You carried rocket flares (in your backpack or in the mast base) to attract attention.

You carried a dayglo flag (taped to the boom) to attract attention.

Smoke flares are of limited use if the wind is strong. The smoke is simply blown off downwind without gaining any height.

Wind Too Light

If you're sailing a sinker, you can get caught out by being unable to waterstart due to lack of wind. There are two alternative courses of action:

Undo the outhaul and, starting at the clew, roll the sail up tight to the mast. Lay the boom alongside, unplug the mastfoot and lay the rig on the board.

You can then lie on top of it and, so long as the wind is light, you will find that a short board is reasonably easy to paddle home.

Alternatively you may be able to get help from a long board sailor. Persuade him to come alongside to windward and then to get in the water so that he can steady your board. You then climb on his board, using it as a platform so that you can lift your rig enough to get a little air. Then step on to your own board and sail home with the long board as escort.

Remedies

The most likely equipment failure is the UJ. Always check it for wear and preferably use the new type which has a steel cable connecting the top and bottom bolts. Always carry some spare line. Harness lines part at inopportune moments.

Paddling home a sinker in calm conditions with flat water is relatively easy. In strong winds and with big waves it may well be quite impossible.

Keeping Fit

Muscles
'unboard sailing requires lynamic effort and all the mus-:les shown in the illustration ire likely to be working during simple manoeuvre like the luck gybe.

However, the most import-int muscles are those in the irms and, in particular, the orearms. They play a major part in hanging from the boom, nanoeuvring the rig, water-tarting and jumping. The nore powerful your arms are, he more dynamic your fun-board sailing is likely to be.

Equipment
nvest in a pair of hand-held nuscle contractors. They are videly available and designed or all sports that involve hang-ng on to something – tennis is in obvious example.

The discipline is simple. With your arms half bent, do hirty contractions in thirty econds – holding the last one or a further thirty seconds. Rest for a minute and repeat he process three to six times over – you can do this two or hree times a day and combine t with other activities such as vatching TV, reading or listen-ng to music.

After two weeks you should be able to increase the number to forty contractions, nolding the last one for forty econds. Go on increasing the number until you reach sixty. Some contractors are fitted vith removable springs so that ou can increase the tension, going back to thirty and start-ng all over again.

A hard session with a con-ractor makes you feel as if 'ou've been hanging from the boom for half an hour.

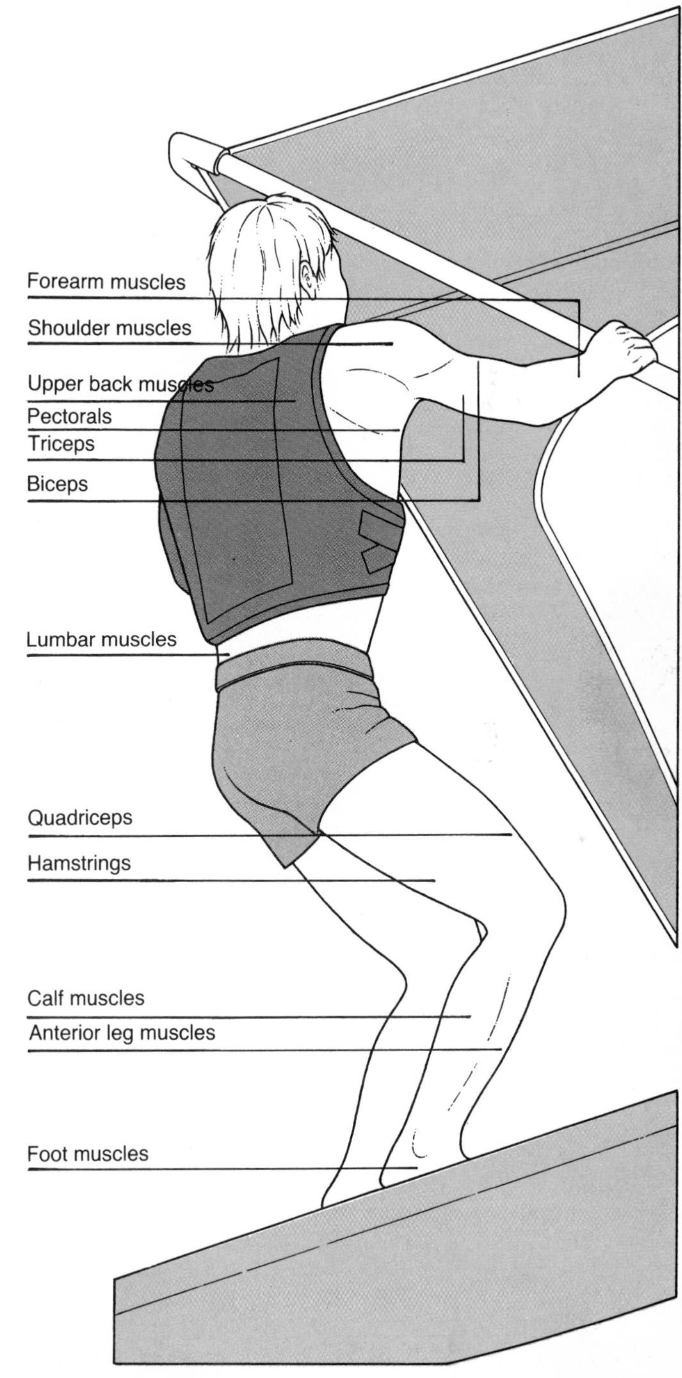

Final Fling

As a finale, there's no better way to cool off or show off than the body drag. It's demonstrated here with cool precision by Swiss ace Charly Messmer.

All you need is a good enough breeze to plane and quite a lot of self confidence.

Blast along on a beam reach, take your feet out of the straps, and step off on to the water front foot first. Follow with your back foot. Let both feet drag while hanging on to the wishbone; keep the rig powered so that the board does not luff up.

Obviously you cannot walk on water forever. After a few milliseconds the board will slow and the rig will threaten to dump you. Before reaching this point, pull down on the wishbone to get your body back to the board and your back knee on the deck. Give the rig a little power and whip on your front foot. Then stand up and sail on.

Glossary of short board gear

A

Adjustable mastfoot
The mastfoot bottom fitting is likely to vary from board to board. The one shown in the diagram bolts into a pair of standard fin boxes. Others bolt into a single fin box, and many have their own patent mast track system.

B

Battens
Glassfibre battens can be extruded in a continuous strip which is cut up into required lengths. However these battens have a high resin to weight ratio (reducing flexibility and durability) and cannot be tapered.

For this reason the best battens are hand made by pressing resin into layers of glass with a finished ratio of around 80:20. The battens must be tapered for the best *bend percentages*. A 27% bend (27% of the distance from the mast) is established as about right for racing; a 37% bend should be used for wave riding and more general sailing.

Hand made battens are unfortunately very expensive, and can add around 15% to the price of a sail. One of the major manufacturers of handmade tapered battens is *Sailbatten*, based in New Germany in South Africa.

Batten ends
Little plastic caps which protect the sail and hold the batten in place.

Without the end caps the battens are likely to make short work of destroying the laminate used in a sail. If you need to cut down the batten length, use a hacksaw and ensure you put the end cap back on.

Boom
Alloy tubes, either round (preferable) or oval. The booms must be light, and also stiff so that they don't open wide when a gust hits the sail – even if they do open they must have enough spring to return to their original shape.

Boom ends
Moulded plastic fittings. Most important is the inhaul end which must fit tightly at the mast with the correct inhaul lashing; a handle is seldom necessary since it is more convenient to hold the mast.

Inhaul fittings vary from manufacturer to manufacturer. Many use the relatively simple *Windsurfing Hawaii* end fitting which relies on a short loop jammed against a knot to make a rock hard inhaul. *Fanatic* have a sophisticated version of the French inhaul method; and *North* and the newest *Mistral* booms have one of the simplest systems which relies on a few turns round the mast.

Boom grip
Most production booms are vulcanised to give a hard wearing rubber finish which is also hard on the hands. Softer grips such as *Progrip* are much more pleasant to hold, but tend to wear through.

C

Cleat
The best are *Clamcleats* which jam a single line. Alloy cleats are much more effective than plastic.

D

Downhaul
Downhaul tension has become increasingly important with more sophisticated rigs. A 4:1 purchase is the minimum amount required to tension the luff of the sail.

Many sailors use a small block and tackle (sometimes standard with more sophisticated sails) which makes it much easier to tension the downhaul.

E

Extensions
High aspect ratio sails require long masts and short booms. An extension is the easiest way to extend the length of a mast – either adjustable (it may interfere with the foot of the sail) or fixed length.

Adjustable booms are also desirable, and much cheaper than needing a different boom for every sail size. They are either telescopic or have removable end sections.

F

Fins
More fins mean increased drag, and long boards tend to rely on a single fin with their tail shapes and rails aiding stability.

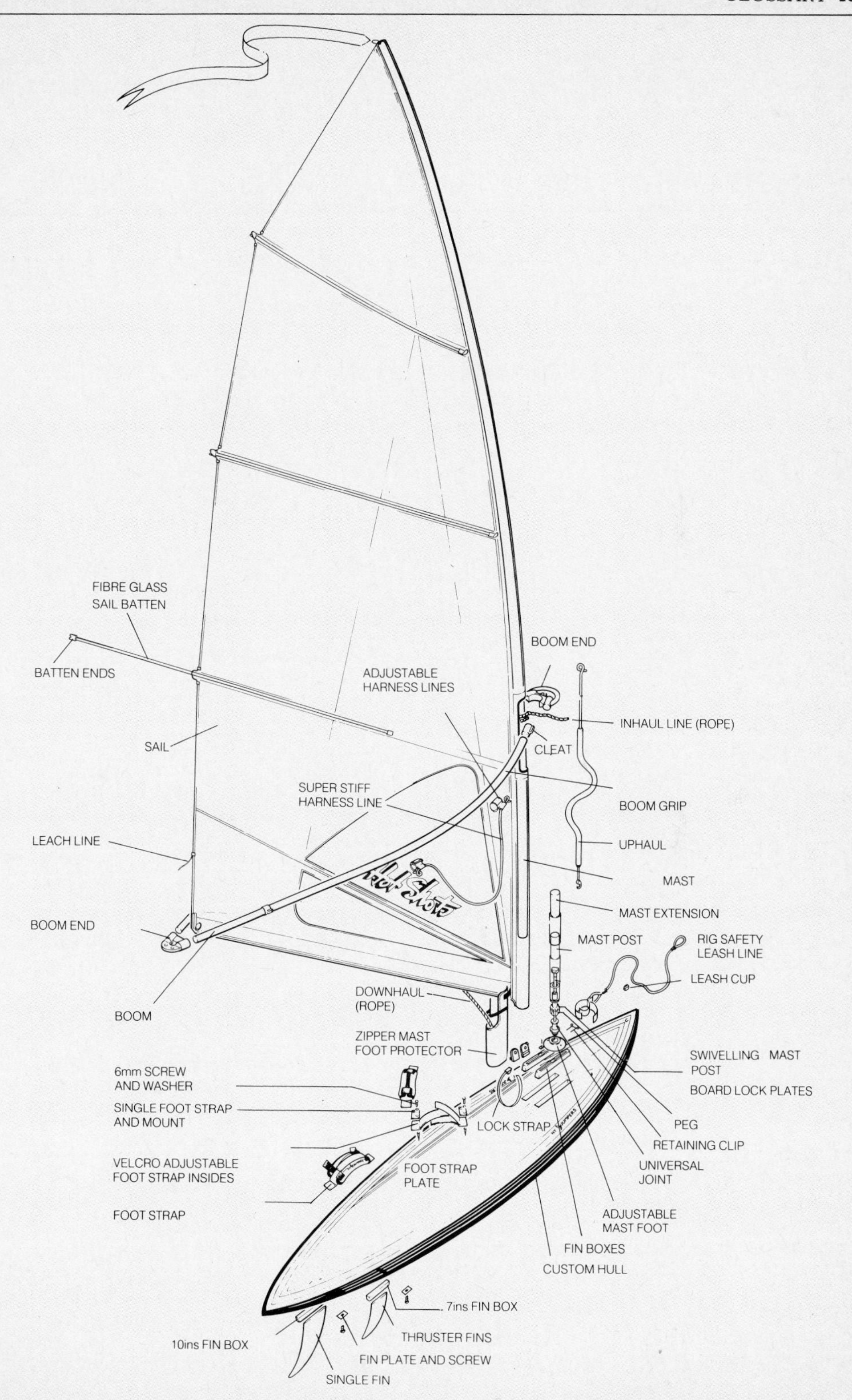
FIBRE GLASS
SAIL BATTEN
BATTEN ENDS
SAIL
LEACH LINE
BOOM END
BOOM
ADJUSTABLE
HARNESS LINES
SUPER STIFF
HARNESS LINE
BOOM END
INHAUL LINE (ROPE)
CLEAT
BOOM GRIP
UPHAUL
MAST
MAST EXTENSION
MAST POST
RIG SAFETY
LEASH LINE
LEASH CUP
DOWNHAUL
(ROPE)
ZIPPER MAST
FOOT PROTECTOR
SWIVELLING MAST
POST
BOARD LOCK PLATES
6mm SCREW
AND WASHER
SINGLE FOOT STRAP
AND MOUNT
LOCK STRAP
PEG
RETAINING CLIP
VELCRO ADJUSTABLE
FOOT STRAP INSIDES
FOOT STRAP
PLATE
UNIVERSAL
JOINT
FOOT STRAP
ADJUSTABLE
MAST FOOT
FIN BOXES
CUSTOM HULL
7ins FIN BOX
THRUSTER FINS
10ins FIN BOX
FIN PLATE AND SCREW
SINGLE FIN

Short boards with wide tails have a single fin with a pair of smaller thrusters out near either rail. They are mostly moulded in translucent polycarbonate plastic – if they are not translucent they are most likely 'glass filled' polycarbonate which is similar in performance.

Hand made 'custom' fins are generally considered to be stiffer than their moulded counterparts. However they are much heavier, and at least twice the price.

Fin boxes
These are also moulded in glass filled polycarbonate and are bonded straight into the board. Thankfully most fins/fin boxes are interchangeable, though the fin should always be a tight fit. Fin boxes are also frequently used as mast tracks.

Fin plate & screw
The plate slides in channels moulded into the box, and the screw holds the fin tightly to it. This allows adjustment of the fin's position: if it is at the front of the box the board is usually 'looser' (more manoeuvrable); if it is at the back it is 'stiffer' (more stable).

Footstraps
The best are adjustable for a wide range of foot or boot sizes; are comfortable with bare feet; and don't flop down on the deck when wet – ie. it's always easy to get your foot in. They are usually made from several layers of overlapping webbing with a thick neoprene outer cover – the whole lot is held together by Velcro.

The straps are normally screwed into mounts which are bonded into the deck. In some cases the straps may be resined directly into a glassfibre hull.

G/H

Handles
The sail should have handles on clew (for tensioning the outhaul); tack (for tensioning the downhaul); and head (for holding the tip of the sail when you're down in a wave).

Harness lines
Usually pre-stretched Terylene of about 5 mm diameter. With short booms of 2.52 m and less 50 cm harness lines are long enough. The ends can be tied to the booms, or alternatively there are fancy Velcro fastenings.

The lines should be stiff. If they show a tendency to flip over inside the boom, try encasing them in narrow plastic tubing.

I

Inhaul line
There are many ways to get a tight fit between boom and mast – usually it depends on the boom end fitting, and we show the simplest method which is applicable to the Mistral and other similar fittings on page 53.

J/K/L

Leash
A leash between rig and board is a great safety factor. Where it attaches at the mastfoot it should allow the UJ to swivel freely, with the other end secured to the nose of the board. If the UJ fails, the rig will then drift upwind of the board and act as a sea anchor.

Lock
Locking a board to a roof rack may seem difficult without a daggerboard case. However you can get board lock plates which fit into a standard fin box and can be locked to the rack with a cable.

M

Mast
Either alloy, glassfibre (made like a fishing rod), or a more fancy laminate such as carbon fibre. Top performance tends to mean a compromise between maximum stiffness and minimum weight. Two-part masts which sleeve together are handy for restricted storage or travelling by aeroplane.

Most manufacturers quote a 'stiffness value' – 6.0 would be very soft, while 8.0 would be very stiff. This indicates the likely deflection of the mast. Makers use sophisticated methods to measure stiffness which involve taking a series of readings of deflection along the length of the mast. Then the sum of the reciprocals is combined to give the final figure.

However, it is possible to calculate the 'stiffness value' quite accurately in the following way:

Support the mast across two trestles, one at its base and the other 1.30 m along its length. At a distance of 4.20 m measure the height of the mast from the ground. Then suspend a weight from this point and re-measure the height.

You can then work out a 'stiffness value' using the formula:

$$\text{STIFFNESS} = 10 - \frac{\text{DEFLECTION (cms)}}{\text{WEIGHT (kg)}}$$

Mastfoot
A complex mass of bits and pieces which holds the rig to the board. Starting at the top, the **mast post** fits into the base of the mast (check that diameters are compatible) and is bolted to the **universal joint** which is bolted at the other end to the **bottom fitting**.

Mastfoot bottom fittings vary from board to board and should be interchangeable – just make sure you keep the nut lubricated so you can change one for another.

N/O

Outhaul
A short line led to a single cleat within easy reach of the boom end is adequate. You must have a clew handle to get enough tension to remove vertical wrinkles in the sail.

If you have problems getting sufficient outhaul or downhaul tension, try using your leg muscles which are much stronger than your arm muscles. Hold the line with both hands, and push away the boom end or mastfoot until the desired tension is obtained.

P

Protector
A padded cover which fits round the base of the mast between the clew of the sail and the deck (about 15 cm). Only really necessary with a glassfibre board which may be damaged if the exposed mast hits the deck with a bang.

Q/R/S

Sails
Choosing the right sail is like finding a path through a jungle. A simple guideline is the shorter the board the shorter the boom. For a board under 3 m you can reckon on needing three sail sizes: 5.5–5.7 sq m for moderate winds; around 4.9 sq m if it's a little windier; around 4 m if it's very windy.

All high performance sails have an outer 'film' which is susceptible to abrasion. If you leave a fully tensioned rig lying on the beach or in the car park, the wind will move it back and fore and sandpaper the film until it is totally destroyed.

For the same reason any high abrasion areas (in particular the head) must be very strongly reinforced; and the boom must not be allowed to touch the leeward side of the sail where it can also rub away the film.

Rotational sails were invented by Barry Spanier and Geoff Bourne as a commercially acceptable version of wing rigs, which are too expensive, too heavy, and much too difficult for most sailors to use.

With a modified luff tube (or luff 'loops') the sail is designed to rotate so that compression from the full length battens (which must be tapered if it is to work) makes it set on the leeward side of the mast.

The result is that there is no turbulence on the leeward side of the sail, which is responsible for most of the drive in the rig as it 'sucks' the sail along.

T

Thrusters
Small side fins either side of the main fin on a wide tailed board. They are there to give more lateral resistance and to make sure something grips the water when the board is banked hard over. They are generally asymmetric (foiled on the outside; flat on the inside) and may be angled in (or 'toed in') towards the nose of the board.

U

UJ
The universal joint is the little rubber joint that holds the mastfoot assembly together and allows the rig to bend where it will. Early ones used to break off, which is a good reason for having a safety leash connected to the mastfoot by a swivel which is above the UJ. More recent UJs have a steel thread connecting their top and bottom threads which is enough to hold the whole lot together in the event of a breakage.

V

Velcro
Used for adjustable footstraps, harness lines, etc. With a lot of use it loses its grip.

W/X/Y/Z

Wax
Rubbed on to the deck to give the board a good non-slip finish. Available from surf and windsurf shops.

Glossary of funboard technique and terminology

A

Aerial
Jumping on the wave face and landing back on it.

Aerial off-the-lip
As above, but performed on the section on the wave which is vertical and about to break. One of the acknowledged masters of this manoeuvre is Craig Masonville of *Hi Tech* who builds asymmetric boards specifically for it.

Asymmetric
A board which has a long pintail on one side for high speed bottom turns; and a short, wide tail on the other side for slow, sharp top turns.

B

Backside
Sailing with your back to the wave.

Beach start/retrieval
The fancy way of launching a long board which was pioneered on the soft sand of Kailua Beach in Hawaii.

Beating
Sailing back upwind, as close to the wind as possible. Funboards either have small daggerboards or none at all, and the lateral resistance of the hull plays an important part in preventing leeway (going sideways).

Blind stitch
A U-shaped stitch used in wetsuit construction. It penetrates only the outside of the neoprene, so that the wetsuit remains fairly water resistant – most of the water that gets in stays in, and is warmed to body temperature.

Body drag
Stepping off the board and stepping back on again – at high speed.

Bottom turn
You sail down the face of the wave and 'bottom turn' to sail back up again. It's invariably performed in a wide arc at high speed.

Break
Literally means when the sea breaks against an immovable object. Thus it can be a 'beach break', 'shore break', 'reef break' etc.

C

Carve
To carve a turn, gybe, or 360, a board must be planing, with the inner rail leaving a 'carved' furrow in the water.

Chop
Small, wind blown waves, generally on inland or sheltered water.

Clew-first
Sailing with the rig back to front so that the clew (rather than the luff) is nearest to the wind. Can be used to keep power on and maintain planing during a gybe; and if you fall off at that point a 'clew-first waterstart' may come in useful.

Close-out
The wave breaks along its entire length and becomes a wall of white water which no-one can sail through. Generally in offshore wind conditions.

Concaves
Designed to promote early planing. However they are a headache for the shaper and the manufacturer, which is a good reason why they are not more common.

Cross shore
The wind blowing from left to right or right to left across the shore will usually mean the best conditions you can get, with easy launching and landing and a beam reach out and back in.

Cut back
Having sailed up the wave after a bottom turn, you 'cut back' to sail back down it.

D

Double concaves
The double concave is the most favoured underwater shape for slalom, course racing, and allround-funboards that have pretensions of speed.

The more sophisticated versions generally combine it with a single concave in the nose area (better floatation and less chance of 'sticking') and 'V' (for better grip) in the tail.

Duck gybe
The 'Whyte gybe' as invented by Richard Whyte in Hawaii – he was just playing about, looking for new tricks.

Duck tack
Part of 'sinker freestyle', and one of the hardest transitions, it requires balance, fitness, and agility.

You carve the board up into the wind; crouch down and reach under the foot of the sail so you can grab the mast on the other side; lean the rig forward; get underneath it; and at the same time pump it to make the board bear away.

Dumpers
Waves 'dump' in a mass of foam when they hit a steeply shelving shore. It's difficult and dangerous to launch in dumpers, which generally happen at high tide.

F

Flaking
Folding the sail with straight creases like a concertina. Film materials don't like being creased, and it is generally better to roll a sail from head to foot – if it's fully battened, it's also much easier.

Footsteering
A planing funboard steers on its bottom and rail shape. You bank it on one side or the other like a water ski, and don't need to steer with the rig.

Frontside
Sailing with your front to the wave, so you're looking at it.

G

Ground swell
Swell (waves) generated by a storm which travels a long way (it could be hundreds of kilometres) before being dissipated when it hits an immovable object, eg land.

Gybes
All planing gybes are 'carve gybes', and the skill is the speed you come out of them, rather than the speed you go into them.

Short boards gybe most easily, while long boards have a tendency to drop off the plane and stop turning – you may have to resort to a 'flare gybe', sinking the tail and weighting the outer rail.

Gun
A board with a long, drawn out profile that has the wide point well forward. Designed primarily to go fast, and describe high speed, wide arc turns.

H

Harness technique
Larry Stanley is owned a lot of thanks for inventing the harness.

The concept has stayed much the same, with the main improvement coming in the use of spreader bars which spread the load across the chest.

Unless you're very sure, it's unwise to hook in when jumping. Some harnesses have a 'crotch strap' which encourages a sitting stance for getting your weight inboard and the rig upright on a long board.

People learning to waterstart like high buoyancy harnesses; but when they master that technique they invariably prefer to sail with less bulk.

Helicopter
Peter Boyde and Peter Cabrinha were among the first to master this 'sinker freestyle' manoeuvre.

The basic technique is to carve the board up and head to wind; pull your body up and over the centreline; and then push the rig away from you. This will get you onto the new tack (with pumping, trimming and a lot of skill). You 'rig steer' the board round on to the new beam reach; and push the clew out through 90° until the wind hits the near side of the sail. It will then flip it through 180° and you can sail off on the new beam reach.

Obviously this manoeuvre is sinky, and is easier on a floaty board. However it's worth remembering that a low volume 2.60 may sink when stationary; but will float when moving at two or three knots which is the sort of speed you'll keep up through this manoeuvre.

J

Jumping
With the right technique you can jump on flat water, lifting the board with your feet and letting the wind get under the hull. From there on it's anything up to twice-mast-high waves of Hawaii.

L

Late drop
The wave is breaking up all around you, and you leave it until the last moment to sail

down the face with white water in pursuit.

Left break
The wave breaks to the left of the surfer.

Lip
The breaking top of the wave.

M

Man-on-man
Two competitors sailing against one another – usually in a waveriding competition; occasionally in slalom.

Mush
Mushy waves tend to be small and break erratically. They are not good for waveriding and not much better for jumping.

O

Offshore
An offshore wind is dangerous for obvious reasons – it gets windier as you leave the protection of the land. Offshore winds tend to 'hold up' waves, which makes for good surfing, and poor windsurfing.

Off the lip
A turn off the 'critical' breaking top of the wave.

Over the falls
Being thrown out by the lip of the wave, resulting in a wipeout.

P

Peeling
A wave 'peels' when it breaks gradually along its length.

R

Reaching
Sailing with the wind on the beam – all funboards are designed for this.

Rip
A severe current which affects the surface of the water and can make difficult conditions.

S

Set
Waves travel as a set, like a platoon of soldiers.

Sideshore
When the wind blows across the shore. Variations are 'side onshore' and 'side offshore'.

Sinker freestyle
Sinker freestyle has evolved from wave contests, and the need to keep inventing better tricks and manoeuvres. Basically, it's just a transition from one tack to the other without using the conventional carve gybe – 'duck tacks', 'helicopters', etc are part of the genre.

Slalom
A high speed competition in which competitors have to gybe round a series of buoys. Gybing technique, acceleration and speed are the three most important qualities for winning. 'Giant slalom' is used for longer course racing boards, combining long reaches with a slalom section.

Speed trials
Seeing how fast you can go over a 500 metre course. The most famous speed trials are held at Portland Harbour near Weymouth every October.

Spin-out
Air gets round the fin so that it loses its grip and the tail slides away from you. Solved by the right design and the right technique, but always a problem when travelling fast in choppy water.

Surfing
Riding a wave, using its speed and the steepness of the face to induce forward motion.

T

Tacking
A transition in which the nose of the board passes through the eye of the wind, and the sailor changes sides by steering round the front of the mast. On short boards tacking is usually impossible, since there is not enough room or volume in the nose.

360
Carving a short board through 360 degrees. Rather than a perfect circle, the board tends to describe a corkscrew spiral. Getting to 180 degrees is relatively simple, but at that point the board often drops off the plane and stops carving – you then have to push the rig forward and pump it to complete the 360 and sail off in the original direction.
(Also called 'unwinding'.)

Top turn
Another name for a 'cut back', a turn made at the top of the wave so you can sail back down the face.

Transition
Changing from tack to tack or gybe to gybe.

Traversing
Sailing along the face of a wave, like traversing the side of a ski slope.

Tuck
The edge of the rail is cut away where it meets the bottom of the board in order to improve water release.

Tube
The lip of the wave throws itself forward and forms a hollow tube. Surfers ride along the tube – a highly skilful pastime.

U

Uphauling
Standing on the board, and pulling up the rig hand over hand, using the uphaul rope. On funboards the waterstart is always much easier.

Upside down jump
Kicking the board up on top of you with the rig hanging underneath. Also called a 'T jump', 'table top', etc.

Ventilation
The same as 'spin-out'.

Waterstart
Getting wind under the rig, and letting it pull you up out of the water and on to the board.

Waveriding
Riding a wave, using its power and speed to increase apparent wind and bump up your own speed dramatically.

Appendices

Weather Forecasts (UK)

Weather forecasts are available on the TV, radio and in the newspapers but are generally designed for people on land. You will learn more from the shipping and inshore water forecasts which are broadcast on the radio and give you the visibility, wind stength in knots or Beaufort Scale and the likely weather pattern.

The principal national daily weather forecasts are as follows:

Time	Broadcast	Station	Frequency
0033	Main shipping forecast	BBC Radio 4	LW & VHF
0038	Inshore forecast	BBC Radio 4	LW
0555	Main shipping forecast	BBC Radio 4	LW
0655	Mon–Fri inshore forecast	BBC Radio 3	VHF & MW
0755	Sat & Sun inshore forecast	BBC Radio 3	VHF & MW
1355	Main shipping forecast	BBC Radio 4	LW
1750	Main shipping forecast	BBC Radio 4	LW

In addition there are extensive local radio forecasts for coastal areas of the UK.

Telephone Forecasts
If you would like specific information you can telephone one of the Weather Centres. Queuing systems usually apply, which means you have to hang on until it's your turn to be answered.

London Weather Centre
01-836 4311
Southampton Weather Centre
0703 28844
Plymouth Meteorological Centre
0752 42534
Cardiff Airport
0446 710343
Manchester Weather Centre
061 832 6701
Glasgow Weather Centre
041 248 3451
Lerwick Meteorological Office
0595 2293
Aberdeen Airport
0224 722334
Newcastle Weather Centre
0632 26453
Suffolk Weather Centre
035 96 466

Alternatively consult your Telephone Dialing Code booklet for the numbers of recorded message weather forecasts. These generally advise on direction and strength of the wind.

The Coastguards will also advise on prevailing weather conditions – you can find their local number in the telephone directory.

Useful Addresses

WSMA
Feldafinger Platz 2, D 8000 Munchen 71, West Germany. Tel: 089 781074. Telex: 5216448 WSMA D.

The World Sailboard Manufacturers Association was formed to run the first World Cup funboard series in 1983. Founder members included many of the major European board manufacturers (Bic, Tiga, Mistral, Fanatic, Sailboard, Hi Fly and F2) and sailmakers (North, Neil Pryde, Hy Line and Gaastra).

In 1984 their numbers swelled to include the sailmakers ITV and Hood and the board manufacturer, Surf Partners. A series of six events was held at La Torche (northwest Brittany, France), San Francisco and Hawaii (USA), Sylt (West Germany), Scheveningen (Holland) and Omaezak (Japan).

The Eurofunboard Cup was also run under the auspices of the WSMA. Eight European regions held their own qualifying events and sent their top sailors to the Eurofunboard Cup held, in conjunction with the World Cup, at Scheveningen.

RYA
Victoria Way, Woking, Surrey, England. Tel: 048 62 5022

The Royal Yachting Association acts as the governing body of yachting in the UK. The RYA has a particularly close involvement with the Weymouth Speed Trials which are held on the 500 metre course in Portland Harbour during October every year.

IWBA
PO Box 1911, Winter Park, FL 32790-1911, USA.
The International Women's Boardsailing Association is predominantly funboard orientated and American inspired. Its achievements include running an IWBA series; ensuring that members could race in the 1984 World Cup; and getting a fair share of prize money at major professional events.

IYRU
60 Knightsbridge, Westminster, London SW1X 7JX.
Tel: 01 235 6221.
The International Yacht Racing Union is the international governing body of yachting, and is responsible for decisions such as choosing the Olympic board.

It is basically 'amateur', and by its very nature tends to have little to do with the overtly commercial aspects of funboard competition.

Speed Sail Association
15 Avenue Pierre Premier de Serbie, 75116 Paris, France. Tel: 33 (1) 723 53 69.
For those who prefer to 'do it on land', the Speed Sail Association runs a European and World Cup each autumn.

Main Events

Hook In and Hold On
Cowpet Beach Hut, Cowpet Bay East, St Thomas, USVI 00802. Tel: 809 775 3325

One of the world's nicest races is the Johnnie Walker sponsored Hook In and Hold On. It takes place in July and is a ten day cruise around the Virgin Islands (Caribbean), which are blessed with constant Force 4 Trade Winds in July.

Mondial Speed
13 Rue de Bellefond, Paris, France.

Speed Trials held on a large coastal lagoon near Sete in the south of France during April.

Brest Speed Week
Dacmar, 20 Rue Danton, 29200 Brest, France. Tel: 98 80 23 95

Brest Speed Week takes place in late September every year.

O'Neill Invitational
O'Neill, 1971 41st Avenue, Santa Cruz, CA 95162, USA.

The O'Neill Invitational is the first big waveriding event of the year held during April at Hookipa Beach on the Hawaiian island of Maui.

British Funboard Cup
PBA, Harts Boatyard, Portsmouth Rd, Surbiton, Surrey, England. Tel: 01-399 2113

The Professional Boardsailors' Association organizes rounds for the British Funboard Cup and UK qualifying rounds of the Eurofunboard Cup.

Weymouth Speed Trials
RYA, Victoria Way, Woking, Surrey, England.
Tel: 048 62 5022.

Generally regarded as the best speed week, and the one where records are broken. It is almost exclusively patronised by boards, with a sprinkling of proas, catamarans.

Summersail Supersailor
Boardsailing Association of South Africa, PO Box 11087, Vlaeberg 8018, 6th Floor, 81 Church Street, Cape Town 8001, South Africa.
Tel: 021 23-3095.

A series of four funboard events held throughout December of each year, and based on Capetown and Durban. Best known is the Gunston Surfsailing International. The 1984 series had a total prize money value of 60,000 rand.

Maui Grand Prix
Ehman Productions, PO Box 479, Paia, Maui, Hi 96779, USA. Tel: 808 579 9765.

The Maui Grand Prix is Hookipa Beach's big autumn (October) waveriding event. Ehman Productions are also involved with the O'Neill Invitational.

Rip Curl Wave Classic
Rip Curl, 101 Geelong Road, Torquay, Victoria, 3228 Australia.

Torquay hosts Australia's premier international funboard event, held during the first two weeks of November.

South West Funboard Cup
Funboard Connection, 11 Burford Road, Forest Fields, Nottingham NG7 6BB, UK. Tel: 0602 786837.

A week long event that follows on from the Weymouth Speed Trials in late October. Based on Cornwall where the north and south coastline give a variety of sailing conditions.

The Beaufort Scale

Admiral Beaufort invented the Beaufort Scale in 1805. The units are knots, which are nautical miles (2025 yards or 1.85 kilometres) per hour. His descriptions are for life on the open sea – it's not quite the same for windsurfing.

Force 0
1 knot or less. Calm. Mirror-like sea.
Force 1
1–3 knots. Light air. Gently scaly ripples.
Force 2
4–6 knots. Light breeze. Small wavelets. May have glassy crests but these will not break.
Force 3
7–10 knots. Gentle breeze. Large wavelets. Crests begin to break. Possibly some white horses.
Force 4
11–16 knots. Moderate breeze. Waves becoming longer with white horses.
Force 5
17–21 knots. Fresh breeze. Moderate waves with white horses and possibly occasional spray.
Force 6
22–27 knots. Strong breeze. Large waves forming with extensive white crests and spray.
Force 7
28–33 knots. Near gale. Sea heaps up and foam from breaking waves blows in streaks.
Force 8
34–40 knots. Gale. Moderately high waves. Edge of crests breaks into spindrift. Well marked streaks.
Force 9
41–47 knots. Severe Gale. High waves. Confused breaking crests. Spray affects visibility.
Force 10
48–55 knots. Storm. Very high waves with long overhanging crests. Sea surface becomes white.
Force 11
56–63 knots. Violent storm. Exceptionally high waves hiding ships from view. Sea covered in white foam.
Force 12
64 knots plus. Hurricane. Air full of driving spray. Very bad visibility.

Results

Speed trials
The present World Record Holder is Fred Haywood (USA) who set an all time best of 30.82 knots at Portland in October 1983.

The only other boardsailor to exceed 30 knots is Peter Bridgman (UK) who ran at 30.08 at Portland in October 1984.

The World Ladies' Record is held by Jenna de Rosnay (USA), wife of Baron Arnaud de Rosnay. She first set the record in 1982; lost it to Marie-Annick Maus (France) in 1983 while having a baby; and won it back in 1984 with a run of 27.2 knots. The world's fastest tandem set a speed of 25.38 in 1983, sailed by Gordon Way and Glen McKinley.
All of these records were set at Portland.

World Cup
The 1983 World Cup consisted of five events, and was dominated by Robby Naish who won all three disciplines (course racing, waveriding, slalom).
1. Robby Naish: USA (Mistral/Gaastra).
2. Ken Winner: USA (Bic/Pryde).
3. Alex Aguera: USA (Mistral/Gaastra).
4. Karl Messmer: Switzerland (Mistral/Gaastra).
5. Kai Schnellbacher: W. Germany (F2/North).

Naish continued his winning ways in the six events of the 1984 World Cup, which also included a classification for women.

1. Robby Naish: USA (Mistral/Gaastra).
2. Ken Winner: USA (Bic/North).
3. Robert Teriitehau: France (Gaastra).
4. Tim Aagesen: Denmark (Mistral/Neil Pryde).
5. Charly Messmer: Switzerland (Mistral/Gaastra).

Women

1. Nathalie Lelièvre: France (Mistral/ITV).
2. Julie de Werd: USA (Bic).
3. Anick Graveline: Canada (Bic/North).

Eurofunboard Cup

The Eurofunboard Cup was held as a series from 1981 to 1983, won by Philip Pudenz, Ken Winner and Karl ('Charly') Messmer respectively.

In 1984 the Eurofunboard Cup was won by Paul Jansen (Netherlands).

Magazines

UK

Boards
196 Eastern Esplanade, Southend on Sea, Essex SS1 3AB. Tel: 0702 582245

On Board
60 Station Road, Draycott, Derbyshire. Tel: 03317 4731

Windsurf
Ocean Publications Ltd, 34 Buckingham Palace Road, London, SW1. Tel. 01 828 1990.

Wavelength (Surfing)
70 Fore Street, Newquay TR7 1EY. Tel: 06373 77505

France

Planche/Planche à Voile
5 Rue du Commandant Pilot, 92552 Neuilly Cedex.

Wind
52 Boulevard de Sebastopol, 75003 Paris. Tel: 277 14 14

Germany

Surf/Funboard
Sachsenkamstrasse 19, Postfach 70 1008, 8000 München 70. Tel: 089 760 0071.

Surfen
Burchardstrasse 14, 2000 Hamburg 1. Tel: 040 3 39 66 – 248.

Netherlands

Surf
Antwoordnummer 1237, 1000 PA, Amsterdam. Tel: 020 5858000.

Windsurf Kampioen
Postbus 93200, 2509 BA Den Haag. Tel: 070 264426

Sweden

Surf Sport
BNL Forlag AB, Box 8184, 104 20 Stockholm. Tel: 08 54 37 10.

Wind Surfin
Stora Nygatan 21, Box 2150, 103 14 Stockholm. Tel: 08 24 17 80.

Norway

Fun Sport
Postboks 5928. Hegdehaugen. 0308 Oslo 3. Tel: 02 46 95 00.

Italy

Surf
Via Tadino 29. 20124 Milano. Tel: 2043813 209341.

Windsurf
Viale Regina Margherita 2 – 20122 Milano. Tel: 02 5924405.

Spain

Surf
San Gervasio de Cassolas, 79 Barcelona 22. Tel: 93 211 11 46.

USA

Sailboarder
PO Box 1028, Dana Point, CA 92629. Tel: 714 496 5922.

Sailboard News
Box 159, Fair Haven, Vermont, 05743. Tel: 802 265 8153.

Wind Rider
1211 Palmetto Avenue, Winter Park, FL 32790. Tel: 305 628 4802.

Windsurf
24581 Del Prado, Dana Point, CA 92629. Tel: 714 661 4888.

Surfer (Surfing)
33406 Calle Aviador, San Juan Capistrano, CA 92675. Tel: 714 496 5922.

Surfing (Surfing)
2720 Camino Capistrano, Box 3010, San Clemente, CA 92672. Tel: 619 485 6535.

Canada

Windsport
550 Bronte Road, 2nd Floor, Oakville, Ontario L6J 4Z3. Tel: 416 827 5462.

Japan

Windflash
Yama Kei, 1-1-33 Shiba-Daimon, Minato-ku, Tokyo.

Australia

Freesail
PO Box 246 Collaroy Beach, 2097 Sydney. Tel: 02 938 3363.

Bibliography

The Complete Guide to Windsurfing
Jeremy Evans (Bell & Hyman)
'The definitive manual for British windsurfers' (The Times). Colour photographs by Alastair Black plus clear and straightforward 'how-to-do-it' drawings. The first half of the book is aimed mainly at beginners; the second half is designed for the more advanced sailor and includes specialist sections by international experts.

The Pocket Guide to Windsurfing
Jeremy Evans (Bell & Hyman)
A handbook of windsurfing techniques using 'how-to-do-it'

drawings ranging from basics to the duck gybe. 'Compact, well produced, and well informed' (*On Board*).

Sailboards Custom Made
Hansi Fichtner (Stanford Maritime) A detailed guide on making your own custom board, but very out of date on design.

La Planche à Voile avec Jenna de Rosnay
Arnaud de Rosnay/Hervé Hauss (Gallimard). Spectacular French coffee-table book on how to become the fastest lady in the world.

Weather Lore for Sailors and Windsurfers
Gunther Roth (EP) Detailed primer on weather by German author.

Dinghy and Boardsailing Weather
Alan Watts (Macmillan) A detailed and somewhat complex book dealing with sailing weather.

Royal Marine Commando 7 Exercises
Cook & Toms (Sphere) An excellent keep-fit regime with a 10 week course that's well suited to windsurfing.

Racing Rules
Published by the World Sailboard Manufacturers Association.

Flying with a Board

Flying with a board and rig can be relatively straightforward. Most aircraft have holds which are large enough; and many airlines are willing to co-operate. However it's worth bearing in mind the following points:

- The travel agent may assure you that it is OK to turn up at the airport with board and rig. It's wise to double check by contacting the customer relations department of the airline concerned, asking them to confirm their agreement by a letter or telex which you can produce at the airport.
- Your board may travel free: or you may be liable to excess baggage; or you may get a hefty freight charge.
- Short boards travel much more easily than long boards, and it may reassure the airline if you refer to a 'surfboard'. Full length masts can cause great problems; it's much easier to travel with a two-part sleeved mast.
- Baggage handlers have little regard for labels which say 'fragile' or 'do not drop'. Cover the board with at least two layers of thick bubblepack. Protect the rails with cardboard or carpet. You can tape the boom and sails to the deck which will protect the board when a few tonnes of cases are piled on top of it. Remember to protect the ends of the mast.
- Get to the airport very early. Either find someone to help you carry the board, or wheel it along on two trolleys which are nose to nose.
- On arrival, customs can be difficult. They frequently demand a deposit which is refundable when you leave the country with the equipment. You should go armed with receipts as necessary.
- Check that your insurance is valid. Even with precautions, boards get damaged and 'disappear'.
- Take plenty of spares, tools, and a basic repair kit if there are unlikely to be many windsurfer retailers at your destination.

Windsurfing Shows

The major windsurfing shows take place in Europe, and are the best showplaces for the sport.

They start in early January with the **London Boat Show** at Earls Court, which is immediately followed by the **Paris Boat Show** at La Defense, and **Boot**, the Düsseldorf Boat Show.

HISWA, the Amsterdam Boat Show, takes place in March, and is followed by **Wind and Surf** at Alexandra Palace in London, an exclusive windsurfing only' show.

All the above shows are open to the public. The most important trade show is **ISPO**, held over four days in early September each year in Munich.

Index

Page numbers in **bold type** refer to illustrations

W

Acknowledgements

Jeremy Evans would like to thank the following who have been a particular help with this book: Arnaud de Rosnay, for writing the Foreword; Cliff Webb who provided the majority of the photos; Sun Star (Canon Cameras) who filled in the gaps; Charly Messmer, Dee Caldwell and Stuart Sawyer who took the time to demonstrate techniques for the photo sequences used in this book; Perry Brewbaker who provided the basics for the wavesailing diagram; Jes Simmons (Bears Board Repairs) who advised on 'Epoxy Repair'; Peter Clark (Scanro), Werner Kuhlmann (Klepper), and Jim Feimster (Alpha) who allowed me to visit their board factories and provided much of the information on manufacturing techniques; Edward Hyde (Hy line) who was a great help on sails and rigs; John Hall (Surf Line) who demonstrated how a top shaper makes a custom board; Chapter who showed how they make custom fins; and Chris Neal Design who provided the Hotshots diagram used in the Glossary.

Final thanks go to Stuart Sawyer who advised on techniques and technicalities throughout the book; to Lesley, who ensured that the book was finished more or less on time; and to Philip Clark and Julian Holland who edited and designed it.

Photo Credits
Where not otherwise credited, photographs are by Cliff Webb. Photographs from other sources appear on the following pages:
Alastair Black: Front cover.
Arnaud de Rosnay: 6-7.
Sun Star: 16, 19, 23 top and bottom, 48, 50, 78-79, 82-83.
Windsurfer bv: 102-103.